Soame Jenyns

Twayne's English Authors Series

Bertram H. Davis, Editor

Florida State University

TEAS 391

SOAME JENYNS
(1704–1787)
Engraving by William Dickinson of the Reynolds portrait. Reproduced by permission of the Trustees of the British Museum.

Soame Jenyns

By Ronald Rompkey
Memorial University of Newfoundland

Twayne Publishers • *Boston*

Soame Jenyns

Ronald Rompkey

Copyright © 1984 by G. K. Hall & Company
All Rights Reserved
Published by Twayne Publishers
A Division of G. K. Hall & Company
70 Lincoln Street
Boston, Massachusetts 02111

Book Production by Marne B. Sultz

Book Design by Barbara Anderson

Printed on permanent/durable acid-free paper and bound in the United States of America.

Library of Congress Cataloging in Publication Data

Rompkey, Ronald.
  Soame Jenyns.

  (Twayne's English authors series; TEAS 391)
  Bibliography: p. 171
  Includes index.
  1. Jenyns, Soame, 1704–1789--Criticism and interpretation.
  I. Title. II. Series.
  PR3519.J45Z87   1984   828'.609 [B]   84-4686
  ISBN 0-8057-6877-7

For Noreen

Contents

About the Author
Preface
Chronology

> *Chapter One*
> The "Poet-Laureate" of the Yorkes   1
>
> *Chapter Two*
> Placeman and Metaphysician   27
>
> *Chapter Three*
> Apostle to the Dissipated   53
>
> *Chapter Four*
> Poetry   72
>
> *Chapter Five*
> Political Writings   100
>
> *Chapter Six*
> Philosophical and Religious Prose   130
>
> *Chapter Seven*
> Conclusion   154

Notes and References   159
Selected Bibliography   171
Index   180

About the Author

Ronald Rompkey studied English at Memorial University, St. John's, Newfoundland, where he received the master's degree. Subsequently, he earned a Ph.D. at the University of London and since then has taught at the University of Victoria, the University of Alberta, the University of Saskatchewan, and lately the University of Lethbridge. He has published a number of articles on eighteenth-century literature and edited *Expeditions of Honour*, the journal and letters of John Salusbury, father of Mrs. Hester Thrale (Piozzi), which were written in Halifax, Nova Scotia, 1749-53. He is currently assistant professor of English at Memorial University.

Preface

We tend to remember Soame Jenyns today as we remember his contemporary, Admiral Byng: for an inglorious moment that overshadowed all he accomplished during his lifetime. As students of eighteenth-century literature will recall, Jenyns fell victim to Samuel Johnson's masterful yet virulent review of his *Free Inquiry into the Nature and Origin of Evil* (1757) published in the *Literary Magazine*. This review has stood ever since as a model of forcefulness and common sense, though unfortunately it has fostered an oversimplified notion of Jenyns as an ineffectual poetaster, wit, and government hack. Jenyns's contemporaries have not altered that notion much. The only contemporary account of his life, an introduction to the collected works (1790) by Charles Nalson Cole, is full of warmth, praise, and admiration. Cole knew Jenyns well, and he speaks of him fondly in his correspondence; yet he lacked in his introduction the detachment to do more than fashion a conventional memorial glancing politely over the details of Jenyns's family history and praising his literary output. Cole's sketch has conveniently guided editors of Jenyns's works and parliamentary historians ever since: to this day we hear the echoes of Cole's assumptions and generalizations. The damage done by Johnson's review and the impressions perpetuated by Cole continue to present us with an imprecise and highly distorted picture of a man who survived over thirty years in Parliament and at the same time made a reputation as a writer of verse and prose.

Our purpose here, then, is to come to a more balanced view of a man who stood at the center of English political and literary life during those seemingly placid years from the fall of Walpole to the introduction of Burke's economic reform bill in 1780. Any man who remains so long in the public eye and who writes so controversially deserves a more precise memorial. The first three chapters of this book will provide a clearer picture of Jenyn's life by carefully documenting the various stages of his career and placing them within the context of the age, paying special attention to the character of the man, the reception of his works, and the nature of his political life. The last three chapters will examine his literary works, beginning with his "Augustan" verse and then moving on to the graceful Addisonian prose that is the hallmark of his essays in the *World*, his political pamphlets, and his speculative tracts.

The life of Soame Jenyns is also interesting as a reflection of an age in which fundamental changes were taking place in taste, politics, and religion. If the truism that minor figures reflect their age more faithfully than men of genius is valid, then certainly Jenyns faithfully reflects those changes, though from a conservative point of view. As he grew older, he continued to admire the literary tradition of the early eighteenth century and dismissed new tastes in writing as an "affectation." Like his contemporary Richard Owen Cambridge, he was what Richard Altick has called a "belated Augustan," one with a respect for an earlier time, one who represented in his declining years the ideals, standards, and habits of thought of the age of Pope and Swift. Jenyns was still writing ironic, witty verse satirizing social behavior in the last years of his life. The same wit provides a playful tone for the satiric essays in the *World* and the pamphlets that stirred his critics to charges of insincerity. With his broad interest in human affairs, Jenyns also soared into the realms of metaphysics, and the same tone occasionally strikes the reader of *A Free Inquiry into the Nature and Origin of Evil*, a thoroughly rational and elegant theodicy that is a typical example of eighteenth-century optimism. The same elegance pervades his *View of the Internal Evidence of the Christian Religion* (1776), a plea for ethical behavior couched in rationalistic language calculated to counter the arguments of deists and freethinkers. It would be plainly unjust to remember such a man with only an occasional dismissive footnote.

I am glad to acknowledge my debt to those individuals who have encouraged and supported me in this endeavor. Patrick O'Flaherty first got me interested in Soame Jenyns. Pat Rogers read the earliest drafts and offered numerous

Preface

valuable suggestions for improvement. The following also made suggestions or read sections of the book in draft: Patricia Morris, M. L. Clarke, David Fleeman, Donald Greene, Bertram Davis, Ian Christie, John Dinwiddy, Evelyn Cruickshanks, Charles Bahmueller, and O. M. Brack, Jr. I wish also to thank the staffs of the Cambridgeshire County Record Office, the Cambridge University Library, the Institute of Historical Research, the Public Record Office, and the British Library. And finally, I could not fail to express my gratitude to the Jenyns family of Bottisham, Cambridgeshire, for their unfailing interest and generosity and to the Social Sciences and Humanities Research Council of Canada for the awarding of research grants that enabled me to bring this book to completion.

Ronald Rompkey

Memorial University of Newfoundland

Chronology

1704 Soame Jenyns born 1 January in London but subsequently raised at Bottisham Hall on the family estate near the village of Bottisham, Cambridgeshire.
1722 Admitted to St. John's College, Cambridge, as a fellow-commoner.
1724 Matriculates at the university. Begins to write poetry.
1725 Leaves the university without taking a degree. Pursues his literary interests in London.
1726 Marries Mary Soame of Dereham Grange, Norfolk. His first published verse, a song, appears in *A Collection of Original Scotch Songs.*
1728 Mother, Lady Elizabeth Jenyns, dies.
1729 *The Art of Dancing.*
1734 Presents a manuscript volume of his early verse, "Poems on Several Occasions. Dedicated to the Rt. Hon. the Lady Margaret Cavendish Harley."
1740 Father, Sir Roger Jenyns, dies, and Soame Jenyns succeeds to the Bottisham estate.
1741 Elected M.P. for Cambridgeshire as a protégé of Lord Chancellor Hardwicke.
1742 Jenyns's wife deserts him in the company of William Levinz, an acquaintance of her husband.
1746 *The Modern Fine Gentleman*
1747 Returned as M.P. for Cambridgeshire. *An Ode to the Hon. Philip Yorke.*
1748 Eighty-seven pages of his poetry published in Dodsley's *Collection of Poems. By Several Hands.*
1749 *The First Epistle of the Second Book of Horace, Imitated. The 'Squire and the Parson: an Eclogue.*
1750 Mary Jenyns gives birth to a son, who apparently dies at birth.

SOAME JENYNS

1751 *The Modern Fine Lady.*
1752 Dodsley brings out Jenyns's first book of poems, *Poems. By******.*
1753 Returned as M.P. for the borough of Dunwich. Mary Jenyns dies.
1754 Jenyns marries Elizabeth Gray. Translates Isaac Hawkins Browne's *De Animi Immortalitate.*
1755 Appointed a lord commissioner of trade and plantations. Contributes five essays to the *World.*
1757 *A Free Inquiry into the Nature and Origin of Evil. Short But Serious Reasons for a National Militia.* Portrait painted by Joshua Reynolds. Samuel Johnson's review of the *Free Inquiry* published in the *Literary Magazine.*
1758 Elected M.P. for the town of Cambridge.
1759 *A Simile.*
1761 *Miscellaneous Pieces, in Two Volumes.* Reelected M.P. for the town of Cambridge.
1764 Lord Chancellor Hardwicke, Jenyns's political patron in Cambridgeshire, dies.
1765 *The Objections to the Taxation of Our American Colonies, by the Legislature of Great Britain, Briefly Considered.* Survives the change of administration.
1767 *Thoughts on the Causes and Consequences of the Present High Price of Provisions.*
1768 Reelected M.P. for the town of Cambridge.
1770 *Miscellaneous Pieces, in Verse and Prose.*
1772 *A Scheme for the Coalition of Parties, Humbly Submitted to the Public.*
1774 Reelected M.P. for the town of Cambridge.
1776 *A View of the Internal Evidence of the Christian Religion.* "America" (also published as "The Pin" and "The American Coachman") appears in several different journals.
1780 *An Ode.* Chooses not to seek reelection and retires from public life.

Chronology

1782 *Disquisitions on Several Subjects.*
1783 Honored by being included in James Barry's mural depicting human progress unveiled at the Society of Arts.
1784 *Thoughts on a Parliamentary Reform.*
1786 The "Epitaph on Johnson" stirs up controversy when it appears in the *Gentleman's Magazine.*
1787 Dies in London, 18 December.
1790 *The Works of Soame Jenyns, Esq. in Four Volumes*, edited by Charles Nalson Cole.

Chapter One
The "Poet-Laureate" of the Yorkes

Family History

One of the most remarkable undertakings in the history of British industry was the draining of a half million acres of bog and silt known as the Fens, a bay of the North Sea of which the Wash is the last remaining portion. For hundreds of years, the sheer size of the undertaking had defeated every previous attempt to do so; but in the seventeenth century, an ambitious project finally succeeded in reclaiming these acres and freeing them for farming and grazing. The most striking part of the project was the draining of a wide tract known as the Bedford Level, an expanse of land taking its name from the fourth earl of Bedford, the chief adventurer of an abortive attempt begun in 1634 under the patronage of Charles I. Though that effort had failed, a fresh start was made in 1649, when a company was incorporated by statute to begin work under the earl's successor. The select body of the corporation consisted of the new earl as governor, six bailiffs, and twenty conservators chosen annually from participating landowners; and after an initial outlay of about £100,000 on capital works, the corporation proceeded with its chief functions, the maintenance of drainage and navigation. These functions involved it in the mundane tasks of dredging rivers and drains and repairing banks, causeways, bridges, and sluices and from time to time required it to take action against private landowners who neglected to scour their drains or remove obstacles. An elaborate bureaucracy composed of a surveyor-general, register, receiver and expenditor general, auditor, serjeant and mace, engineer, and assorted superintendents and sluice-keepers took care of such matters, but two of these influenced the work of the corporation more fundamentally. The surveyor-general bore the burdensome and laborious responsibility of submitting proposals for draining works and attending to their execution; the receiver and expenditor general received the taxes laid upon adventurers' lands, took in rents due the corporation from its estates, disbursed salaries to the officers, and paid the interest on bonds. In fact, the latter handled all the financial affairs. While the works advanced in Cambridgeshire and parts of the five adjacent counties, the Fen Office was actually situated in London, first at the Inner Temple and then in Fleet Street.[1]

One of the first adventurers who met near Temple Bar in 1649 and contributed to the costs of having the act passed was Roger Jenyns of Hayes, Middlesex, an ambitious businessman who later moved up in the hierarchy of the corporation when he was elected conservator in 1663 and then bailiff four years later. From that time onward, he and his family seem to have profited substantially from the venture, and in 1673 Roger Jenyns obtained a seat at March in the Isle of Ely. He served as surveyor-general of the corporation from 1686 until his death in 1693, when he handed over the superintendency of the works to his elder son, John, who in turn fulfilled these duties until his own death in 1715. His younger son, Roger, served as receiver from 1689 to 1725. Thus, the Jenyns family was instrumental in the early development of the Bedford Level, and a Jenyns continued to sit as conservator or bailiff until well into the nineteenth century. The two sons of Roger Jenyns flourished, and the Jenynses took their place as one of the influential and respected landed families in Cambridgeshire. John Jenyns represented the county in the parliament of 1710 and held the seat until his death. His brother Roger, though he never sat in Parliament, exerted his influence during elections, when he apparently gave his support to the Tories. William III honored the latter with a knighthood at the turn of the century, and as an appropriate place to display his arms, Sir Roger soon purchased the manor of Allingtons and Vauxes, a substantial estate near the village of Bottisham, midway between Cambridge and Newmarket, an estate that has continued as the Jenyns family seat to this day. When the parish was enclosed in 1801, this estate spread over 1,400 acres. The ancient manor house Bottisham Hall, replaced in the eighteenth century, sat within about 140 acres of park divided by an avenue, belts, and plantations. Around the house ran a garden and a moat, and its admirable interior featured a library as well as a chapel with images of the twelve apostles adorning its windows.[2] Though no trace of the original house remains, the Reverend William Cole of Milton, the Cambridgeshire antiquarian, judged it to be "one of y. neatest and pleasantest Summer Situations in y. whole County."[3]

Two conflicting assessments of Sir Roger Jenyns survive. The admiring Charles Nalson Cole praised him as "an upright, knowing, and diligent magistrate, a great encourager of industry, and at enmity with vice and its parent idleness; a constant promoter of good and orderly government, both by precept and example."[4] However, the Reverend William Cole found him to be "an artfull, cunning & intriguing Man" who advanced his own interests by his own cleverness and good management.[5] Sir Roger was twice married but found some difficulty in producing an heir. His first wife Martha, a widow, shared with him the house he had built at Ely near the bishop's palace and gave birth to a son and two daughters who died in infancy. When Martha herself died suddenly in 1701, she was buried in the south transept of Ely Cathedral. A year later, Sir Roger married Elizabeth Soame, the daughter of Sir Peter Soame, Bart., of Heydon, Essex, in what was to be the first alliance between the two families, and the ceremony was performed by the bishop of Ely in Ely Chapel. From contemporary accounts, Lady Jenyns seems to have been intelligent, polished, and religious, a striking feature of Sir Roger's household at Bottisham and in London, where he worked regularly at the Fen Office. She too miscarried the year after the marriage, but during a trip to London in 1703, she finally gave birth to her only child, who was named Soame Jenyns. She died in 1728 at the age of sixty-two and was buried in the family vault at Bottisham parish church. According to Sir Roger's family notes preserved at Bottisham Hall, she left £100 to purchase land for a charity school for the children of Bottisham and the adjacent parish of Swaffham Bulbeck, and her husband subsequently erected such a school to teach twenty children as a memorial to a woman known for her many acts of virtue and charity.

And so Soame Jenyns was born a Londoner late on New Year's Eve, 1703/4, demanding that his parents choose a birthday for him. Though his mother recorded the time of his birth as "halfe an houre after ten,"[6] the register of the parish of St. Giles-in-the-Fields proclaimed that the date was "the i Instant," and New Year's Day was adopted as his birthday thereafter. According to Charles Nalson Cole, these events used to amuse Jenyns in later life when it came time to celebrate a birthday. Biographers, said Jenyns, carefully recorded the circumstances surrounding the birth of their subjects so as to show how they portended the lives those subjects would eventually lead. He himself had been born in the midst of controversy, and he found all controversy disagreeable. But unfortunately, Soame Jenyns could not avoid controversy: his gift for polite ridicule and his espousal of controversial political and philosophical ideas denied him the sequestered life he might have preferred. Indeed, the portents were correct.

Jenyns grew up surrounded by the splendors of Bottisham Hall and the natural beauty of the Cambridgeshire countryside, developing at an early age two lasting tastes: literature and country life. His mother took charge of his early education and then handed him over for private instruction to two local clergymen, first the Reverend W. Hill and then the Reverend Stephen White, vicar of Swaffham Bulbeck, who directed his studies until he reached the age of seventeen.[7] Then, in 1722, he was admitted to St. John's College, Cambridge, a college of Tory and Anglican sentiment and at the time the largest in the university, admitting annually an average of fifty students. He took up residence as a "fellow-commoner" under the tutelage of Dr. William Edmundson, one of the college's more distinguished senior fellows, and willingly accustomed himself to the university routine for more than two years.[8]

The fellow-commoners were a privileged circle, sons of noble or county families or of rich men, and they were usually exempt from attending lectures and performing most of the exercises imposed upon undergraduates. Comfortably placed in most instances, they could afford to practice extravagance and idleness, and their privileges undoubtedly encouraged them to adopt bad habits. The authorities tended to overlook their breaches of discipline or to punish them mildly, but if a fellow-commoner wished to take a degree, they required him to perform the necessary acts (unless exempted by right of birth). Most of them happily departed the university without doing so.[9] Soame Jenyns matriculated in 1724 and departed the following year, unconvinced that the degree was either necessary or exacting.[10] According to custom, he left as a gift a cup of silver gilt that is still preserved there, and in *World* no. 177 facetiously drew on his experience in describing the university education of "Sir Henry Prigg," a young squire not unlike himself who in two or three years acquired "the usual advantages of that sort of education, such as the arts of sporting, toasting, billiards, and coachmanship," sufficient qualifications to introduce himself into "the best company; that is, the company of smarts, bucks, jockeys, and gamesters."[11]

Forsaking the customary Grand Tour, Jenyns now took up residence in London during the winter months and indulged his literary interests. He argued, stayed up late, and gamed; but already he had begun to toss off a verse or two, and the hallmarks of his maturer work, his correctness and wry humor, can already be observed at this stage. If Pope was his model, Prior was his muse. Here is a formal piece of amatory verse, "To a Lady in Town, Soon After Her Leaving the Country," that anticipates the mocking, ironic satire to follow in later years:

> Restless sometimes, as oft the mournful dove
> Forsakes her nest forsaken by her love,
> I fly from home, and seek the sacred fields
> Where CAM'S old urn its silver current yields,
> Where solemn tow'rs o'erlook each mossy grove,
> As if to guard it from th' assaults of love;

> Yet guard in vain, for there my CHLOE'S eyes
> But lately made whole colleges her prize;
> Her sons, tho' few, not PALLAS cou'd defend,
> Nor DULNESS succour to her thousands lend;
> Love like a fever with infectious rage
> Scorch'd up the young, and thaw'd the frost of age,
> To gaze at her, ev'n DONNS were seen to run,
> And leave unfinish'd pipes, and authors—scarce begun.
>
> (1:116–17)

With its circumlocution, conventional diction, and classical allusion, it is a clever piece of comic verse. What is typical of Jenyns here is the tone of detached amusement, a common feature of his verse and the reason critics have often dismissed him as a "wit" rather than a "poet." Jenyns's playful side may also be observed in another early poem, "The Picture" (1727), preserved by the Reverend William Cole with a note informing us that the source of inspiration was a Miss Belle Williams, sister of the public orator of Cambridge, whom Jenyns observed singing in the choir of Ely Cathedral:

> Her Shape's so genteel, & so pretty her Size,
> Such rosy red Lips, & such rolling black Eyes.
> So white is her Bosom, & her Waist is so small,
> 'Tis enough to charm Bishop, Dean, Prebends, & all.
> Her hand is so soft, 'tis the highest of Bliss,
> From the Tip of her Finger to ravish a Kiss.
> With her Head on one Side, & a languishing Eye,
> She murders in Earnest, in seeming to die.[12]

During the years after he came down from the university, Jenyns turned out a variety of such light verse, and around 1730 he brought some of them together in a manuscript volume entitled "Poems on Several Occasions. Dedicated to the Rt. Hon. the Lady Margaret Cavendish Harley,"[13] a selection of songs and love poems that would appear later in various published collections. In the meantime, he attracted public attention with *The Art of Dancing*, his first poem of substance.[14] A parody of the "art" poem written in a mock-heroic vein, it progressed pleasantly through its three cantos, at once an historical treatise on dancing, a handbook of drawing room etiquette, and a guide to the folk dance.

At the instigation of Sir Roger, Jenyns was married in 1726 to a woman from Norfolk, but the marriage was a disaster from the start. The illegitimate daughter of Colonel Edmund Soame of Dereham Grange, Norfolk, a soldier who had died in 1706 at Torbay as he was leaving on an expedition to Spain, Mary Soame was a woman with "a very bad Complexion, lean scraggy Arms, & no Ways inviting."[15] Yet she had one redeeming feature: on the death of Colonel Soame's sister in 1710, she had inherited the principal portion of her father's fortune. The executrix of the will was Lady Elizabeth Jenyns.[16] Sir Roger encouraged this marriage of convenience without much consideration for the feelings of the two people involved, for according to Jenyns's friend, the Reverend William Cole, no one imagined there was much affection between them. Nevertheless, in May 1726, the marriage took place at Burwell in the diocese of Norwich, a church in the possession of the University of Cambridge,[17] and the bride brought a handsome dowry of £10,000. For fifteen years the two tolerated each other. Then, in 1742, two years after Sir Roger's death, Mary Jenyns eloped with the philanderer William Levinz, M.P. for Nottinghamshire, with whom she is supposed to have dealt on familiar terms while Levinz was staying as a guest at Jenyns's house,[18] and with the allowance of a separate maintenance, she established herself in London. In 1750, she gave birth to a son, who probably died in childbirth.[19] When she herself died in 1753, she was honorably buried in the family vault in Bottisham church.[20]

After a decent interval of a few months, Jenyns next married his cousin Elizabeth Gray, whose mother was another daughter of Sir Peter Soame. She had been living at Bottisham Hall as a "housekeeper," causing what the Reverend William Cole calls "early Differences" between Jenyns and his wife. The vicar of Bottisham conducted the ceremony in the chapel of Somerset House on 26 February 1754. Cole regarded the offer of marriage as a magnanimous act on Jenyns's part, even though the couple had shared the same house during the intervening years; for, he said, "she is a Person of no great Beauty now, whatever Pretensions she might have had formerly, which I have often heard say she had, & likewise pretty far advanced in years, & no Fortune at all to make up Deficiencies: which, tho' Mr. Jenyns wants not, yet as he is rather of a niggardly & covetous Disposition, would no Doubt have added much to her Recommendation." The mild-mannered Elizabeth Jenyns, however, was well liked. To Jenyns, she was a sympathetic and devoted companion, and he remained devoted to her for the rest of his life. Cole informs us that several of the "soft & tender Things" in his poems are meant as compliments to this lady, "who is indeed very deserving of them, so far as an easy, good & complying Temper can entitle her to them. . . ."[21]

As Jenyns approached thirty, he was settling comfortably into the role of squire and man of letters, spurning the usual raucous delights of the country and visiting London from time to time for mental stimulation. In his "Epistle to Lord Lovelace" (1735), we may catch some notion of the tastes he had developed even though the poem is tinged with self-ridicule throughout. Because, he says, he is bored with the pursuits of the gentry, "seldom I with 'squires unite, / Who hunt all day and drink all night." Instead, his interests being primarily literary, he is more apt to spend his time

> with a book or friend:
> The circulating hours dividing
> 'Twixt reading, walking, eating, riding;
> But books are still my highest joy,
> These earliest please, and latest cloy.
> (1:45)

Such an existence, of course, also lacked a focus. Jenyns was not trained in a profession, and until his father died, very few responsibilities fell to him. The rural life of a bookish young gentlemen was far removed from the pursuits of the country gentry, and thus there is a hint of something less than complete happiness in these lines:

> 'Tis thus, my lord, I free from strife
> Spend an inglorious country life;
> These are the joys I still pursue,
> When absent from the town and you;
> Thus pass long summer suns away,
> Busily idle, calmly gay.
> (1:48)

By 1741, that style of life had changed completely. The year before, Sir Roger had died, and his remains had been placed next to those of his wife in Bottisham church, where a handsome monument stood in his memory. Soame Jenyns had inherited his father's entire fortune. More significantly, he had accepted the invitation of the Cambridgeshire Whigs to let his name stand for Parliament, unexpectedly beginning a long public career that would disrupt the even tenor of his way.

Cambridgeshire Politics

We cannot fully understand the nature of Soame Jenyns's political career without reference to county election practices. For a would-be politician, the chief political asset in the eighteenth century was the ownership of land. Tenants were expected to vote according to the instructions of the landlord or his agent, and, with such a pattern long entrenched, the counties came to be regarded as the perogative of landed families. Political history was the history of the exchange of property and family rivalry,[22] and there was no better example of this than Cambridgeshire, a county in which the smaller landed familes who had traditionally exercised control gave way to the aristocratic families of Yorke and Manners. Previously, less influential families such as the Jenyns family had undertaken the duties of parliamentary representation as a responsibility, much as they had undertaken those of the county magistracy. A term at Westminster completed the education of a country gentleman emerging into public life. And just as freehold carried with it the vote, the larger estates carried with them a seat in Parliament for a number of years. With the advent of these two large, powerful families, however, this principle began to break down. The landed families quickly realized that if an estate of a certain size could send a representative to Parliament, it could also mean that an estate of twice that size could return two members.[23] That, at any rate, is how the Yorke and Manners families construed it. Once established on their newly acquired lands, they viewed the county as a legitimate political battleground and exercised their primacy over it for over sixty years.

Certain influential Cambridgeshire estates had historically maintained their political importance irrespective of the families who possessed them from time to time. One of them was Wimpole, a center of political activity since the reign of Henry VI. In 1720, the distinguished Harleys acquired it and for a time shared the representation of the county by virtue of their ownership. When the powerful Lord Chancellor Hardwicke purchased Wimpole in 1739, however, he not only purchased property but established a political base as well and assumed the right to control county politics, so that in the elections of 1741 and 1747, the electoral pattern changed dramatically. Previously, no family had returned both members for the county at the same election.[24] Family tradition still carried more weight than party affiliation, and county affairs received more attention than national or international issues. But Hardwicke was very much a national figure, and his interests lay outside the county. Cambridgeshire was merely one of his many political fiefdoms.

Hardwicke had first entered Parliament in the Commons and quickly ascended to the top of the judiciary. From 1740, he exercised the controlling power in the government and exhibited it strikingly when he defended Walpole's administration against the attack by Cartaret and helped defeat the ensuing motion of censure. During the king's absences, he used his influence as a member of the council of regency, and he added to his prestige as the confidant and mentor of the powerful duke of Newcastle. His eldest son, Philip Yorke, extended the family influence. From 1747, Yorke sat for Cambridgeshire, and from time to time he received minor political appointments. He was styled "Viscount Royston" in 1754. Members of the Rockingham administration met frequently at his town house, and he himself briefly entered the cabinet in 1766 after succeeding to his father's title.

The Yorkes first tested their influence in Cambridgeshire during the election of 1741. Lacking sufficient time to present their own candidates, they continued to support candidates put forward by the county families: in this case, the incumbents Samuel Shepheard and Henry Bromley. But that year, Bromley was created Baron Montfort, and the two failed to find a single member of the gentry to support their interest after thoroughly canvassing the county for a replacement. Distressed by so many refusals, they eventually turned to Soame Jenyns. Jenyns would not have stood high on their list, for by now he had become a beauish individual, not properly equipped to join in the raucousness of electioneering. Some suspected him of being a Tory. These obstacles detained the Whigs only briefly, however, for they soon concluded that Jenyns at least possessed the right qualities to be a government member, if not a politician. As the Reverend William Cole observed, "they conceiving well of this Gentleman's good Sense & Integrity, were thoroughly satisfied in their Choice: for he saw that the keeping up of Parties was only a political Contrivance of a Minority, in order to make themselves considerable & be taken notice, yet always avail themselves of every Occasion that offers itself to serve their own Interests."[25] Jenyns did not appear to be the best choice for a candidate, but the choice was slim and the local organizers at least felt sure of his loyalty. By the next election, the Hardwicke interest would be fixed more firmly and better prepared. For the time being, a candidate had agreed to stand. When the election passed without incident, in June 1741 Jenyns accompanied Samuel Shepheard to Westminster, though for much longer than anyone would have predicted. From that time onward, he continued to support the faction in power, a practice regarded suspiciously as tergiversation by other members, but he insisted that because he held no fixed political views, except for his general dislike of opposition, he could reconcile his opinions with the policy of any government leader.

As Jenyns adjusted to the more urbane life of London society and politics, the nature of his poetry changed fundamentally: the light, amorous verse of his youth gave way to a more incisive comic satire of manners. The first poem published after his election, one of the best he wrote, was "The Modern Fine Gentleman" (1746), a lively and perceptive "character" poem based on his observations of the would-be politician, the fop, the parasite, and the gamester. Here, for the first time, he demonstrated a talent for gentle, mocking verse and an understanding of the ironies of the social scene. His aspiring young gentleman, having burst upon the world in a fit of passion and ambition, fails at everything he tries:

> And now arriv'd at his meridian glory,
> He sinks apace, despis'd by Whig and Tory;
> Of independence now he talks no more,
> Nor shakes the senate with his patriot roar,
> But silent votes, and, with court-trappings hung,
> Eyes his own glitt'ring star, and holds his tongue.
>   (1:69)

The ever watchful Robert Dodsley was impressed by this effort, and the same year he himself published three more, the "Epistle to Lord Lovelace" and two poems from the manuscript volume presented to Lady Margaret Cavendish Harley, in the second voume of the *Museum*. Suddenly, Jenyns's name was being recognized in a modest way outside the political sphere.

By the election of 1747, Jenyns was no longer a reluctant novice but an experienced political ally of the Yorkes, who by this time were well established in the county—so strong that Philip Yorke now prompted the faltering Samuel Shepheard to retire from his county seat and make room for Yorke himself. Shepheard resented the dismissal at first, but he later accepted the offer of a seat for the town of Cambridge, holding it until his death the following year. The Yorkes offered the other county seat to Jenyns, who had carried out his duties in such a respectable manner that they were happy to retain him. But when the Yorkes decided to mount an energetic and expensive campaign, Jenyns soon discovered his distaste for the arduous business of going about among the sometimes boisterous voters and entertaining them. He found it tedious and boring; yet he managed to keep up with Philip Yorke during the round of public meetings, and once again the voters did not spare their enthusiasm. The results seemed to justify the extravagant election expenses heaped upon them when they returned the two with a comfortable majority. At the end of the campaign, Yorke wrote to Thomas Birch, "I rode into the Town at the head of a fine Squadron of 600, & I believe Mr Jenyns was not attended wth a less number. Our Side of the County never exerted themselves better to do credit to themselves & their Candidates."[26] Relieved at the outcome, Jenyns rushed out with "An Ode to the Hon. Philip Yorke," a defense of political life that described campaigning as a necessary evil. He wrote,

> A man, when once he's safely chose,
> Should laugh at all his threatening foes,
>   Nor think of future evil:
> Each good has its attendant ill;
> A seat is no bad thing, but still
>   Elections are the devil.

The poem concluded with a sketch of the two candidates and a frank confession by the poet, who now found himself to be a permanent part of the Whig interest in Cambridgeshire:

> The gods to you with bounteous hand
> Have granted seats, and parks, and land;
>   Brocades and silks you wear;
> With claret and ragouts you treat,
> Six neighing steeds with nimble feet
>   Whirl on your gilded car.
>
> To me they've giv'n a small retreat,
> Good port and mutton, best of meat,
>   With broad-cloth on my shoulders,
> A soul that scorns a dirty job,
> Loves a good rhyme, and hates a mob,
>   I mean who a'n't freeholders.
>   (1:133–35)

The following year, the poem appeared in *The Foundling Hospital for Wit*, a collection of light verse edited by Sir Charles Hanbury Williams.

Jenyns received even more recognition as a poet when Dodsley decided to print a selection of his verse in *A Collection of Poems. By Several Hands* in January 1748 and turned what Horace Walpole called "a paltry poet"[27] into one of the most widely read poets in England. Dodsley's *Collection* was not necessarily the best critical selection that could have been made at the time, but it was a fair representation of poetic taste, and it made available poems still read today (including poems by Gray and Johnson) though not yet collected in a popular form. Besides three of Jenyns's standard satiric poems, there were four from the manuscript volume and three new ones, including "An Essay on Virtue," his first attempt at philosophical verse. "An Essay on Virtue" owes something to Pope's *Essay on Man* by adopting the doctrine of plenitude in the universe and of a "chain" of creatures culminating in God (see chapter 6), a "parent, guardian, friend" who has created a "sportive nursery" for our enjoyment. By implication, it attacks Christian ethics with the assertion that man is naturally good and need only follow the dictates of nature to be happy in the short time he has in this world. Jenyns would expand these ideas later, but for the moment this was his most ambitious poem since "The Modern Fine Gentleman," and Gray took the trouble to praise it in a letter to Horace Walpole.[28] With so much of his poetry now in print, Jenyns was more apt to be recognized in London as a man of letters than as a member from the shires.

Soon there were three more satiric poems. "The First Epistle of the Second Book of Horace, Imitated" was a "burlesque imitation" written in 1748 and dedicated to the lord chancellor. A discourse on English election practices, it reveals how the traditional role of the county families was changing and how men of all ranks were presuming to put their names forward for election. Without losing its playful tone, the poem becomes a lament for a more settled style of county politics in which the outcome was usually taken for granted. Whereas this poem followed faithfully the pattern of its Horatian original, the next departed from Jenyns's customary procedure by commenting critically on contemporary political events.

After the defeat of the Jacobites in 1745, the Young Pretender had again taken refuge in France, and the war in Europe had dragged on without a decisive action until the powers signed an inconclusive treaty at Aix-la-Chapelle in 1748. By this time, the national debt had grown to alarming proportions, and the government leader, Henry Pelham, was so uneasy about the high rate of inflation that for the next six years he pursued a policy of peace and retrenchment. At the time of the signing, Jenyns produced "The 'Squire and the Parson: An Eclogue," an amusing dialogue between a country parson and his Tory squire that ridiculed certain opposition attitudes. "There is some humour in this little piece," Ralph Griffiths noticed in the *Monthly Review*, "which is partly intended as a burlesque on the country gentlemen of WESTERN'S kidney."[29] We find the squire reading the Jacobite *London Evening-Post*, complaining of the high cost of living and the deterioration of his holdings, and gruffly blaming the state of the country on "fetching Hanoverian kings." The parson, who laments the influence of "purblind Reason" among the faithful and the onset of "free-thinking" and other attitudes influenced by the French Enlightenment, scorns the squire for his apparent disloyalty but capitulates eagerly when the squire threatens to withhold the living the parson is expecting to receive at his hands. As a study in political attitudes, it showed a different side of Jenyns's talent but one that was by no means exhausted.

Superior to both of these was "The Modern Fine Lady," published by Dodsley in February 1751 and already into its third edition by April. Compared to "The Modern Fine Gentleman," it does not quite measure up; but it does succeed as a grim portrait of the young "Lady Harriott," who adopts a fashionable mode of life full of coquetry and cards and sinks peevishly into a decline. Beginning with her frivolous life in the city, the poem then moves to the country in a Hogarthian "progress." This poignant history of pride frustrated soon established itself as one of Jenyns's standard pieces. Gray mentioned to Walpole soon after it was published that "The Fine Lady has half-a-dozen good lines dispersed in it"; and Hester Thrale (Piozzi), a girl at the time, recalled in 1804 how in one particular passage "Pope never crack'd the Kernel of Life, & tasted with more poignancy the Bitter Core— than did Soame Jenyns in those pungent Verses."[30] Jenyns's elegant verse was attracting attention, and his satiric touches stood out favorably against those of other minor poets.

Dodsley was not long in recognizing this, and in 1752 he decided to publish a volume of Jenyns's verse because, he suggested in the advertisement, "it is now thought proper to collect them together, revised and amended, with the addition of several others by the same hand." Under the title *Poems. By******, Jenyns's name nowhere appeared, but a large urn on the title page bore his arms and motto. The poet's name was no secret anyway, for as Ralph Griffiths pointed out generously in his review, "The public is already so well acquainted with the poetical abilities of this very ingenious gentleman, that it cannot be thought necessary for us to give any other than a short specimen of the present collection; and that only for the sake of such of our readers as have not seen Mr. *Dodsley's* three volumes."[31] All the poems Dodsley had published previously and the longer poems were now collected together with several more from the manuscript volume and thirteen others not seen before. Dodsley was shrewdly taking advantage of Jenyns's apparent popularity. Even superior poets who would continue to be read when Jenyns was forgotten did not share this distinction yet. As Sir Egerton Brydges recalled, "While Soame Jenyns and Paul Whitehead were among the favourites of their day, poor Collins was committing to the flames, in indignation, the solitary impression of those divine Odes, which no one would buy or notice!"[32] For the time being, readers still enjoyed traditional "Augustan" verse, and for as long as a taste for it lasted, these mocking perceptions of social and political practices continued to sell.

As Jenyns was savoring his newfound literary reputation in London, a second powerful aristocratic family challenged the Yorke monopoly in Cambridgeshire. When the sixth duke of Somerset died in 1748, his extensive estates were divided between his two daughters. The portion allotted to his daughter Frances Seymour included the seat at Cheveley and much of the adjacent property, which subsequently became the seat of the Manners family when in 1750 Miss Seymour married John Manners, marquis of Granby and the son of the third duke of Rutland. Manners rapidly built Cheveley into a second political center that remained in operation almost until the introduction of the Reform Bill in 1831,[33] during which time the electoral history of Cambridgeshire became the history of the rivalry between the Yorke and Manners families. It began at the next election and immediately put an end to Soame Jenyns's tenure as a representative of the county.

The politics of the two families were so similar that in the beginning they might have discovered some common ground through compromise and run Cambridgeshire as a peaceful coalition, but instead they chose independent paths. In 1753, the intractable Lord Granby disappointed the Whig leadership when he declared he would never join Hardwicke in either expense or interest and proceeded with Lord Montfort to set about courting the Cambridgeshire Tories. As the election approached, Granby mustered his supporters about him, many of them freeholders averse to the Yorke monopoly—men who were deserting one family to support another whose intentions were similar yet not so obvious. When Granby announced he would run in the county himself, he immediately placed Jenyns's seat in jeopardy, and the Yorkes plucked Jenyns from the race. Jenyns was disillusioned, but his parliamentary career was not finished yet. Hardwicke, who was fond of him, though not so fond as to underwrite a futile campaign, intervened at this point and explained to Philip Yorke,

> I don't know whether You have yet seen M.r Jenyns. I don't wonder he is uneasy; tho' He has no reason to be so in respect of a Seat for himself in Parliam.t, for he will certainly be taken care of. I think I have observed that part of his Uneasiness has arisen from a dislike of being laid aside for the County, & a dissatisfaction with my Lord Montfort; &, as the Event draws nearer it operates stronger. And yet when He is talk'd clearly with, He cannot argue, or suppose, that it is reasonable that Things should go on upon the unequal foot they were upon. However it is our Business to keep him in as good humour as possible. I have a real Regard & love for him, & will never give way to any thing, that shall carry any slight towards him.[34]

As a result, the Whigs compensated him with £600 from the "secret service fund" and provided him with a safe seat in order to clear the way for a compromise between Yorke and Granby. (Membership in a party per se was unknown at this time, and political factions guaranteed the loyalty of their members by such emoluments. Jenyns continued to receive compensation until he accepted a patronage appointment to the Board of Trade in 1755.) At Montfort's suggestion, Sir Jacob Downing offered the great Whig manager, the duke of Newcastle, his seat in the rotten borough of Dunwich for £1,000, whereupon the seat was purchased for Jenyns and the cost divided between Newcastle and Jenyns himself.[35] Granby, a popular figure, heavy with military achievements, won the election in Cambridgeshire with Yorke unopposed, and the two repeated their success in 1761. Soame Jenyns, however, never represented Cambridgeshire again.

A Portrait of the Man

At this point, we might usefully ask what kind of person Jenyns had turned into during his maturer years and how he impressed his contemporaries. For certain, he was not an easy man to forget, and there is no shortage of information from those who knew him. To begin with, he was not a handsome man, and he compensated for his uncomely appearance by affecting a dandyish mode of dress peculiar to itself and by cultivating a fine vein of good humor and wit that endeared him to his friends and exasperated his adversaries. No one could fail to notice Mr. Jenyns's appearance or his eccentricities. The Reverend William Cole thought his poetic treatise on dancing appropriate because his friend resembled so much a dancing master and gave odds that anyone ignorant of his station in life would guess the same thing. Samuel Johnson, ventured Edmond Malone, was thinking of Jenyns when he created in *Rambler* no. 24 the character of "Euphues," whose ambition it was "to distinguish himself by Particularities in his Dress, to outvie Beaus in Embroidery, to import new Modes, and to be foremost in a new Fashion."[36] Richard Cumberland, who shared many a hilarious evening with him, summed up his appearance best in later years:

He came into your house at the very moment you had put upon your card; he dressed himself to do your party honour in all the colours of the jay; his lace indeed had long since lost its lustre, but his coat had faithfully retained its cut since the days, when gentlemen embroidered figured velvets with short sleeves, boot cuffs and buckram skirts; as nature had cast him in the exact mould of an ill-made pair of stiff stays, he followed her so close in the fashion of his coat, that it was doubted if he did not wear them: because he had a protuberant wen just under his pole, he wore a wig, that did not cover above half his head. His eyes were protruded like the eyes of a lobster, who wears them at the end of his feelers, and yet there was room between one of these and his nose for another wen that added nothing to his beauty; yet I heard this good man very innocently remark, when Gibbon published his history, that he wondered any body so ugly could write a book.[37]

Jenyns was so ugly, in fact, that when Richard Sheridan's sister met him at a reading party given by Mrs. Vesey a year before he died, she judged him to be "the most hideous mortal" she had ever beheld.[38]

Imagine the amusement, then, when he sat a month and a half for Joshua Reynolds in 1757 and took home one of Reynolds's characteristically inoffensive half-length portraits of himself accoutred in his lace ruffles and wig. "It is the most flattering Likeness I ever beheld," remarked the Reverend Mr. Cole when he saw an engraving of it in later years (see the frontispiece), "& tho' it was never like him that I remember, which is near 50 years, yet one can't say it is altogether unlike: the Prominency of the Eye, tho' that is much softened, gives it the Resemblance." When Cole sent a copy to Reynolds's friend Horace Walpole, Walpole agreed. "It is proof of Sir Joshua's art," he replied, "who could give a strong resemblance of so uncouth a countenance without leaving it disagreeable."[39]

Nevertheless, he was a thoroughly likeable and pleasant individual, and he gained entry to the London salons because of his unflagging wit and sense of humor. He could turn the most unremarkable incident into an object of mirth and enliven an evening assembly with drollery while somehow managing to avoid giving offense. His amusing conceits were heightened further by the "inarticulate" way he spoke through his broken teeth.[40] Richard Cumberland describes his sense of humor precisely:

His pleasantry was of a sort peculiar to itself; it harmonized with every thing; it was like the bread to our dinner; you did not perhaps make it the whole, or principal part, of your meal, but it was an admirable and wholesome auxiliary to your other viands. Soame Jenyns told you no long stories, engrossed not much of your attention, and was not angry with those that did; his thoughts were original, and were apt to have a very whimsical affinity to the paradox in them . . . though his wit was harmless, yet the general cast of it was ironical; there was a terseness in his repartee, that had a play of words as well as of thought, as when speaking of the difference between laying out money upon land, or purchasing into the funds, he said, "One was principal without interest, and the other interest without principal." Certain it is he had a brevity of expression that never hung upon the ear, and you felt the point in the very moment that he made the push.[41]

It was good-natured, epigrammatic humor that lacked malice. Long after he died, Hannah More illustrated his good temper by telling the story of the friend who paid a call and accepted Jenyns's offer of a slice of cold meat, only to be told by a servant that there was not a scrap left. When the servant had left the room, Jenyns turned to his friend and said, "Now we had a large round of beef dressed yesterday; this is therefore rather unaccountable. But I expect these things; and that I may not be subject to lose my temper, I set down £300. a year to losses by lying and cheating, and thus I maintain my composure."[42] The transfer of conversation into print, of course, is always a risky business. Inevitably, the sense of the occasion dims with the passage of time, the impact of the rejoinder or pun wears away, and what seemed funny to a contemporary goes flat. Nevertheless, so many contemporaries have remarked upon Jenyns's wit that it seems to have been his most obvious public feature, particularly in the House of Commons.

Jenyns indeed enlivened the long sittings in the House of Commons, but not with his oratory. Speaking through broken teeth in an inarticulate manner is not the best way to stir an assembly. His talents were better applied elsewhere. "He twice endeavoured to speak in the House of Commons," remembered Edmond Malone, "and every one was prepared with a half-grin before he uttered a word; but he failed miserably. He had a most inharmonious voice, and a laugh scarcely human."[43] The shafts of aphorism were more likely to strike at smaller committee meetings, sittings of the Board of Trade or evening parties. When, for instance, in 1763 Parliament entered a long debate on the ordnance and seemed as if it would remain preoccupied with it until the end of the session, Jenyns suggested the following motion: "Resolved, that this committee has spent *its* time as foolishly as the nation has done *its* money."[44] This typifies the trivializing tendency of his humor, it seems, and Benjamin Franklin took note of it one evening after a dinner at Lord Shelburne's, where there had been a discussion about easing the restraints on paper money in America. Franklin expected a repeal, but he also expected some difficulty with members of the Board of Trade who had signed the report restricting it, for, as he remarked, "there was a good deal in what Soame Jenyns had laughingly said when asked to concur in some measure, *I have no kind of objection to it, provided we have heretofore signed nothing to the contrary.*"[45] Horace Walpole, Jenyns's parliamentary opponent, was often present on such occasions, and he delighted in relaying these bons mots to his correspondents. On the practice of "pairing" with a member of the opposition during debates, he reported to William Mason, "Seeing some members pairing off in the Speaker's chamber, he said, 'I think there are no happy pairs now in England, but those who pair here.'"[46] Finally, government members often used to tell the story of an appeal sent to Jenyns by his friend Richard Owen Cambridge upon meeting the African traveler "Abyssinian" Bruce. When Cambridge found out Bruce was to dine at Lord North's, he solicited an invitation and consequently heard many strange revelations, including the suggestion that Bruce had sent camels to America. Struck by the novelty of this, Cambridge immediately dispatched a letter to Jenyns at the Board of Trade asking whether the board had received any information about the importation of camels: "Jenyns delayed his answer a few days and then wrote to him that many had arrived in America, but their names were spelt differently, Campbells."[47]

Jenyns's gift for seeing the ridiculous sometimes landed him in trouble when anonymous satires appeared. He was accused of writing the well-known *Tar-water, A Ballad: In-*

scribed to the Rt. Hon. Philip Earl of Chesterfield. When *An Ode to Sir Charles Hanbury Williams; Occasioned By Seeing An Ode to Lord Chesterfield* came out in reply, the watchful Horace Walpole suspected him immediately; but Jenyns never acknowledged it, and the ode cannot be found in a single edition of his works. Two other inflammatory pieces were attributed to him in 1773. First, he was one of those suspected of writing William Mason's "Heroic Epistle to Sir William Chambers," an attack on the king and court. Enjoying the anonymity, Mason kept the mystery alive but could not implicate Jenyns to his satisfaction. Reporting a conversation with Lord Holdernesse, he wrote, "I ventured to say that I thought it worthy of Soame Jennyns had it suited his political sentiments. He replied, 'So it was, but S. J. would never have used that *harsh* kind of satire.'"[48] Next, Dr. Burney's *Present State of Music* called forth the parody *Musical Travels in England*, by "Joel Collier." Some readers ascribed it to Jenyns, and Boswell thought he noticed that "a slight attempt is made to ridicule Johnson," who had long ago attacked his *Free Inquiry*.[49] But the target was clearly Dr. Burney, Johnson's personal friend, and there was no evidence to implicate Jenyns this time either. In later years, the same suspicion arose again when a parody of Johnson ridiculed his relationship with Mrs. Thrale. When Mrs. Thrale's husband died, some suspected that Johnson desired to marry her himself and for that reason showed his disappointment when she married Gabriel Piozzi, her daughters' singing master. The incongruous idea of Johnson's amorous intentions again incited the wits, and pieces of verse started to emerge in the popular press, like this one imitating Johnson's ponderous style of speech:

> Cervisial coctor's viduate dame,
> Opinst thou this gigantick frame,
> Procumbing at thy shrine,
> Shall catinated by thy charms,
> A captive in thy ambient arms
> Perenially be thine.

Mrs. Thrale could think of only one person with both motive and wit to write it,[50] but she could never prove that he had.

Jenyns's opportunity did not come until after Johnson was dead.

Meanwhile, one or two celebrated pieces of satiric verse did backfire and draw down upon the unfortunate poet almost as much attention as the poems themselves. In 1758, Jenyns sent off to Hardwicke a piece of light verse for his amusement, warning him not to show it to anyone but those who might "properly" peruse it. So amusing was it, that the sheet got handed around among the Whigs, and by February 1759, what had begun as a private joke at the Tories' expense had found its way into the *London Chronicle* and other newspapers under the title "A Simile." The poem drew attention to the government action of 1757 and 1758 by which Pitt had sent troops and finances to the Germans—especially to Frederic of Prussia, with whom the British had signed the Convention of Westminster in 1756. Observing the country gentlemen of the Tory opposition acquiesce in these measures, Jenyns compared them to a country lass who at first guards her virtue and then loses it by degrees to a sophisticated army officer, concluding, "They're fairly sous'd o'er head and ears, / And cur'd of all their rustic fears" (1:201). At this time, Jenyns was regarded not only as an exponent of the Whig viewpoint but the recent author of the *Free Inquiry*. The following week, a savage *ad hominem* attack came out in the *Monitor* from somewhere within the Whig camp, applauding Pitt's achievements and defending the understanding shared by Pitt and the Tories as a step essential to the security of the country. It mocked Jenyns as the author of the *Free Inquiry* for attempting to prove "the *necessity of corruption*" in the governors of a free country and for exercising his talent for ridicule against those who had attempted to "revive a military spirit in a great and once warlike people." Then it retaliated with the "fragment" of Doll Common, a country girl who loses her sense of shame until

> At length she comes upon the Town;
> First palms a Guinea, then a Crown;
> Nay, Slander says, that underhand,
> The forlorn Wretch would walk the *Strand*;

> 'Till grown the Scorn of Man and Woman,
> A Pot of Beer would buy *Doll Common*.[51]

It was the most vicious attack made publicly on Jenyns to that point, and it made much of his recent sinecure appointment to the Board of Trade. The attacker's name remained a mystery until a year later, when Thomas Birch informed Royston in confidence, "the Writer of that Monitor is a Clergyman, who since the preferment, which he receiv'd from you, has been courting it elsewhere by several political pieces in favour of a great Minister."[52] He was the Reverend John Brown, author of the controversial *Estimate of the Manners and Principles of the Times* (1757), whom Hardwicke had presented to the living of Great Horkesley in 1756. When Hardwicke learned of his activities, Brown resigned. The affair had caused Hardwicke a great deal of trouble, for when Sir John Philips reproached Pitt again during the ensuing debate on the Corn Bill, Pitt had had enough, and according to Horace Walpole, it required Hardwicke's "intercession and protection" to save Jenyns's place at the Board of Trade.[53]

In 1780, another fugitive piece ruffled feathers again, this time in the literary world. As a man of conservative tastes, Jenyns resented experiments in poetic form, particularly the irregular Pindaric ode. Though now well advanced in years, he could not resist indulging himself in the delights of a burlesque imitation of this form innocently titled "An Ode," and it brought him far more trouble than he expected. It opened with a speech from "the giant Gogmagog," who is supposed to have gone mad from some disappointment in ambition or love. Suddenly, there followed an apostrophe to the sun and then one to the moon and an unexpected shift to four descriptions of the seasons. The "ode" then concluded with an address to Liberty, ridiculing practitioners of the ode and parliamentary reformers at the same time:

> Hail, Liberty, fair Goddess of this isle!
> Deign on my verses, and on me, to smile;
> Like them unfetter'd by the bonds of sense,
>   Permit us to enjoy life's transient dream,

> To live, and write, without the least pretence
> To method, order, meaning, plan, or scheme:
> And shield us safe beneath thy guardian wings,
> From Law, Religion, Ministers, and Kings.
> (1:220)

Important to an understanding of the sarcasm here was the poem's preface, a "learned" discourse that explained in particular the unlikely transitions and lack of method. "These rules," it said, "have been observed with great diligence, and some success, by most of the writers of modern Odes; but have never been adhered to with that happy exactness, as in the piece which is now before us." This part in particular aroused Walpole, the self-appointed custodian of Gray's reputation, who took it as an attack on Gray and William Mason, "our only Pindars." Already incensed by Johnson's comments in his life of Gray, he pressed Mason for a reply and would not rest until Mason satisfied him in 1782 (see p. 65, below) with "The Dean and the 'Squire: a Political Eclogue" under the pseudonym "Malcolm MacGreggor."[54]

More celebrated than any of these, however, was Jenyns's unfortunate "Epitaph on Johnson," lines spontaneously written for private amusement but mysteriously communicated to the *Gentleman's Magazine*. Once more they brought the retired placeman before the public gaze. Jenyns did not bear any malice toward Johnson for his review. As William Bowles told Boswell, Johnson particularly enjoyed receiving marks of respect from those he had injured, including the few kind words from Jenyns after his illness in 1783.[55] But at an evening's entertainment at which the party were making up extemporary epitaphs, Jenyns could not resist the temptation to employ his fabled wit against him in his absence. Here is what he wrote:

> Here lies SAM JOHNSON:—Reader, have a care,
> Tread lightly, lest you wake a sleeping Bear:
> Religious, moral, generous, and humane
> He was; but self-sufficient, proud, and vain,
> Fond of, and overbearing in dispute,
> A Christian, and a Scholar—but a Brute.
> (1:222)

Afterward, these rough lines were quickly put away and forgotten. Johnson died the following year, and immediately his intimates began the task of collecting his opinions and treasuring up anecdotes. First, Mrs. Piozzi's *Anecdotes of the Late Samuel Johnson LL.D.* (1786) aroused the curious, and the entire first edition quickly sold out. It was a new approach to biography, for Mrs. Piozzi had dared to show Johnson's blemishes. To the puzzled reader, nearly every admiring statement she had made seemed to have been contradicted in the later pages. Johnson's loyal friends, particularly Boswell, rushed to his defence; for weeks social chat ranged over the merits of the various rival biographers, and the papers blossomed with facetious verses and epigrams. A month after the publication of *Anecdotes*, Jenyns again felt his fancy quicken. He revised his epitaph and sent off a copy of this more caustic version to his bluestocking friend, Mrs. Boscawen, who in turn showed it to Mrs. Delany, one of those constantly horrified by Johnson's outbursts of rudeness. It concluded,

> Would you know all his wisdom and his folly,
> His actions, sayings, mirth and melancholy,
> Boswell and Thrale, retailers of his wit,
> Will tell you how he wrote and talk'd and cough'd and spit![56]

When this version found its way into the *Gentleman's Magazine*, it caused consternation among Johnson's friends. "It was an unbecoming indulgence of puny resentment," fumed Boswell, "at a time when he himself was at a very advanced age, and had a near prospect of descending to the grave."[57] Unable to control his anger, he came back with a vicious reply "*Prepared for a Creature* not quite dead *yet*," a performance completely different in spirit from Jenyns's. The same year, John Courtenay continued the counterattack with an insulting review of Jenyns's career, trivializing his literary accomplishments.[58] Once again, Jenyns stayed quietly chastened and never bothered to answer these rebukes, for by now he had grown accustomed to the consequences of his own wit.

Chapter Two
Placeman and Metaphysician
The Board of Trade

When Soame Jenyns received an appointment as one of the lords commissioners of trade and plantations in 1755 in reparation for the loss of his Cambridgeshire seat, Britain had entered a period of political uncertainty that lasted until the end of the Seven Years' War in 1763. At home, the death of the government leader, Henry Pelham, had created a vacuum difficult to fill, while at the same time the conduct of foreign affairs had grown steadily graver. In Europe, though Newcastle had negotiated a series of treaties designed to contain France, the Anglo-French rivalry had extended to North America. In India, the truce of 1748 had been broken. These events promoted the rise of William Pitt, a gifted minister of Pelham's cabinet who had fully expected to succeed his leader but who had been passed over in favor of his rival, Henry Fox. Pitt believed in Britain's greatness as a trading nation and held a concept of empire based on Britain's trade potential. He therefore attacked Newcastle's foreign policy and urged stronger support for British colonists in North America. If necessary, he said, Hanover—Britain's Achilles heel on the European continent—should be sacrificed to preserve American interests. For these independent views, he had been dismissed from the cabinet, but the Seven Years' War hastened his return.

The chief means of communication with British overseas interests at that time was an ad hoc committee of Parliament known as the Lords Commissioners of Trade and Plantations (commonly known as the "Board of Trade"), a body established by William III in 1696. The board possessed no executive powers but merely advised the government about matters placed before it by individual entrepreneurs. Prior to 1724, it had acted vigorously, but its zeal abated when Newcastle chose to neglect colonial business, largely because Sir Robert Walpole had decided not to interfere in the development of the colonies. By the middle of the eighteenth century, the number of its meetings had dropped to only ten a month.[1] When the earl of Halifax became president in 1748, however, it began to take its duties more seriously again, mainly because Halifax, through his personal ambition, had won the right to correspond directly with the colonies and control patronage. By the time Soame Jenyns attended his first meeting, the board had regained its place as a significant part of the general strategy of the government. From time to time, it numbered among its members such figures as the earl of Halifax, the earl of Dartmouth, Thomas Pelham, Richard Rigby, Bamber Gascoyne, Edward Gibbon, Hans Sloane, and a variety of other lesser-known noblemen and members of Parliament. Yet none of them remained at the board for long, and the members usually drifted away to other things.[2]

Jenyns was a rare instance of a politician who accepted his appointment as a sinecure and then remained a member for twenty-five years, conscientiously attending meetings and absorbing himself in commercial interests overseas. The appointment at first caused some dismay on the opposition side. Horace Walpole, an inveterate enemy of the Yorkes and an M.P. who had entered Parliament at the same time as Jenyns without managing in the meantime to secure a place of any kind, jealously reported, "The Duke of Newcastle, the Duke of Bedford, the Chancellor, and a little time afterwards Mr. Fox, had each a nomination to the Board of Trade, and placed there their friends, Judge Talbot, Mr. Rigby, Soames Jenyns, the poet-laureate of the Yorkes, and young Hamilton."[3] To a certain extent, Walpole was justified in his cynicism, for he had applied regularly to each ministry, only to be refused each time. He took pleasure in singling out Jenyns's membership in his indignant assaults on subsequent ministries and in later years moved on to belittle his writings with the collaboration of William Mason. Jenyns, for his part, enjoyed his good fortune, and he took pains to affirm his allegiance to Newcastle by informing Hardwicke, "I now want but one thing in the World, wch is an Opportunity of shewing my Gratitude & Devotion to his L^p . . ."[4]

During Jenyns's twenty-five years at the board, as Britain passed through a phase of considerable commercial expansion, the members remained in touch with every part of the expanding empire through its supervision of trade. Merchants, fishing entrepreneurs, slave traders, wine dealers, land speculators—all of these came to the board with recommendations, and the board, though it possessed no executive, financial, or penalizing powers, determined the degree of their success to some extent through its reports to the crown and its correspondence with colonial governors until after the Seven Years' War. No agency was more mercantilist and none more protective of the king's prerogative in America. In promoting trade, it promoted the interests of the mercantile classes. Its membership was drawn from nobles and landowners, men who moved within a fixed orbit of thought and who interpreted the world in terms of Britain's welfare. Their reports were full of recommendations upholding the conventional point of view that the colonies should remain dependent on the mother country so as to provide a source of wealth for her people.[5] Nevertheless, when Halifax resigned as president in 1761, the board's prestige abated substantially, and the gains made by Halifax—the power to control correspondence and the power to make nominations to colonial offices—slipped away. Merchants and manufacturers subsequently learned to deal with Parliament directly, so that in later years, when the Americans revolted, all communication with the American colonies had ceased, and the board had lost its principal source of business. Although Lord North separated it from the American Department in 1779 and advised colonial governors to work through it directly, this was merely an empty gesture to mollify a subsequent president, the earl of Carlisle. By this time, advocates of parliamentary reform were seizing upon its virtual inactivity as an example of the

North ministry's imprudent waste of funds, for it was obvious that the board members were not fruitfully employed. Richard Cumberland called it "an office of no great labour," and Gibbon confessed, "it must be allowed that our duty was not intolerably severe, and that I enjoyed many days and weeks of repose without being called away from my library to the office."[6]

When, in 1780, Burke introduced into Parliament five bills designed to abolish such sinecure places and refloat the civil list, he provoked one of the liveliest debates of the session. Time after time, he returned in his speech to the 2,300 folio volumes of reports submitted over the years by such distinguished members as Locke, Addison, and Prior and reaffirmed their uselessness. While he admired the distinguished members, he described the board itself as "an academy of Belles Lettres" in which every department of literature had its separate professor. Seizing upon Jenyns's reputation as a writer who had published a book on the subject of evil, he mocked him publicly, asserting that "the hon. gentleman's long experience might have led him to know that the Board of Trade was one great political evil . . . one of the greatest political evils, or indeed the aggregate of them all."[7] The case had been effectively put. The lords of trade, Gibbon tells us, "blushed at their own insignificancy," and when the vote was taken, the motion carried 207 to 199.[8] As luck would have it, all other clauses of the bill were substantially defeated, and the board managed to survive until 1782, at which point it was dismantled. But the occasion marked the end of Soame Jenyns's career in Parliament. The embarrassment and ridicule were more than he could tolerate, and shortly thereafter he resolved to have nothing more to do with public affairs. Throughout his long association with the board, as we shall see, he had heard the same argument used against him many times.

The Nature of Evil and Samuel Johnson

In the year of the appointment to the Board of Trade, Soame Jenyns's literary reputation rested solely upon his poetical works. That year, he first exhibited another side of his ability—an elegant and polished prose style—in five numbers he contributed to the *World*, the periodical conducted by Edward Moore the dramatist between 1753 and 1756. He published almost exclusively in prose from that point onward. The *World*, in spite of the brevity of its existence, was one of the most popular ventures of its kind, and its success may be attributed to its considerable snob appeal. At its zenith, it claimed a circulation of 2,500 and numbered among its contributors Lord Chesterfield, Lord Bath, Sir Charles Williams, William Whitehead, Richard Owen Cambridge, Francis Coventry, Horace Walpole, and Jenyns himself: men of "rank and genius" by whose reputations it intruded into the upper circles of society, places of privilege withheld from its forerunners. Unlike the more intellectual papers such as the *Rambler*, it offered few serious subjects and avoided criticism. Religion and politics were forbidden. Instead, it proclaimed that its design was "to ridicule, with novelty and good-humour" the "fashions, follies, vices and absurdities" of society, a preoccupation for which Jenyns was admirably suited by inclination and ability. His contributions are examples of clarity and sustained irony in the Addisonian manner, the equal of any other in the collection.

There is an assumed hauteur about these five papers. They confine their attention to such subjects as the aspirations of the lower classes, the social activities of the country gentry, and the pride and laziness of servants. Number 178 is a portrait of "Sir Harry Prigg," a gentleman who does not seem to have noticed how boring he has become since his "elegant retirement" to the country, and number 163 is a discourse on the transmigration of souls. Periodical essayists had previously treated this last topic as a matter of fun and ridicule, and in fact the reader might have readily mistaken this paper as another instance of the same sort of treatment. Surprisingly, Jenyns claimed in the opening lines that it had been "always a favourite of mine" and appeared to take it seriously. It was his first attempt at rationalist philosophical prose, anticipating ideas that would appear again in later works. Undoubtedly, it must have appeared curious to those readers accustomed to his subtle humor. And when later he shifted from the *jeux d'esprit* of the *World* to the weightier *Free Inquiry into the Nature and Origin of Evil* in 1757, his colleague Gerard Hamilton was not the only one to wonder how someone with "no notion of ratiocination, no rectitude of mind" should write such a book. Jenyns was not known as a systematic thinker. "If however there was anything weak, or defective, or ridiculous in what another said," Hamilton continued, "he always laid hold of it and played upon it with success."[9] More than one reader noted this apparent contradiction in attempting to understand what was behind the *Free Inquiry*.

The question of why evil exists in the world has always been a central problem in Christian theology, particularly because evil cannot easily be reconciled with the supposed actions of a benevolent God. This question became increasingly poignant in the eighteenth century in the light of theories advanced by the New Science, theories that had changed men's way of looking at the world. The implications of new scientific ideas had intrigued philosophers since the time of Locke, and the *Free Inquiry* was one of a great corpus of treatises, pamphlets, essays, and sermons published as the controversy gained momentum (see chapter 6). There were four editions in the first year alone. Though Jenyns was not regarded as an original thinker, the *Free Inquiry* was a very clear and well-ordered amalgam of the arguments advanced by rationalist writers over the previous fifty years.

Appearing in the garb of an empiricist, Jenyns granted the existence of an omnipotent and benevolent God and took as his task the objective of reconciling "the miseries we see and suffer" with that benevolence. The thrust of his argument was that evils owe their existence to "necessity": that is, they could not have been prevented without the loss of a superior good or the permission of a greater evil. Consequently, we can see that evil is not inconsistent with the power and goodness of God. Things are all right the way they are, he seemed to say. What we perceive as "evils" are merely elements of a grand plan we are privileged to glimpse only in part. In adopting this position, Jenyns had adopted the theory of the eighteenth-century optimists grounded in the concept of a universe disposed as a "Great Chain of Being," a system of subordination in which every creature was supposed to have its appointed place and men were "as happy as their respective situations permit." These concepts appear significantly in Locke's *Essay Concerning Human Understanding* (1690) and later merge with the optimism of Archbishop King, Bolingbroke, Leibniz, and others. One of the most articulate and popular statements of them was Pope's *Essay on Man* (1733-34), a work that directly inspired Jenyns, particularly in its conclusion that social evils and inequalities were also "necessary" and not subject to change.

By 1750, no satisfactory answer to the problem of evil had been put forward by rationalist thinkers—not even by the deists. The empiricist method borrowed from scientific enquiry had been tested, particularly by David Hume, and had been found wanting. Christian apologists had grown so used to deistic arguments that by 1757 counterarguments had sprung up from every quarter. Thus, when Jenyns's book appeared, the critics frankly found it difficult to take the author seriously, for an ironist and wit was now expounding with apparent facility those philosophical ideas they considered patently absurd. Jenyns's declaration about the "necessity" of evil reminded William Rose in the *Monthly Review* of newspaper "Nostrum-Advertisements," and Rose wondered whether, if the words "*Theological-Powder, Tincture,* or *Electary*" were substituted and the effects described, it would expose the author's perceived vanity and pretension. The dissenting polemicist Caleb Fleming, writing under the pseudonym "Philagathos," could not make up his mind on first reading whether "hidden satire" did not lurk beneath the surface and in the end was still not sure whether the book was a "burlesque on infidelity." Thomas Gray called it "the little wicked book about Evil" and found nothing in it but absurdity; Richard Shepherd thought Jenyns gave "too great scope to the wild flights of his own fancy," and another anonymous Christian pamphleteer agreed.[10] Though the work sold well, Jenyns's timing and his reputation as a wit undermined its serious intention from the start. Even more attention was paid its defects because Samuel Johnson chose to write about it. In Boswell's view, Jenyns had "ventured far beyond his depth" and found himself exposed by Johnson's clarity.[11]

Johnson's review in the *Literary Magazine* was so devastating and vehement that it has virtually determined the cast of Jenyns's literary reputation to this day. While few readers take the trouble to acquaint themselves with what Jenyns actually *said*, every serious student of Johnson has examined the review and weighed it both as a model of ironic criticism and as an historic final blow to the theory of the Great Chain of Being as a philosophical principle (see chapter 6). Yet whatever the nature of his argument, Johnson was as skeptical as the other reviewers about Jenyns's seriousness, and he directed much of the rhetorical fervor of his attack at the man and his literary career rather than the work at hand. Seizing, for example, upon Jenyns's fantasy of a race of superior beings somewhere in the universe who perhaps interfere in the affairs of men further down the chain of being, Johnson turns it against the author himself in this account of the publishing successes hitherto fostered by Dodsley:

They now and then catch a mortal proud of his parts, and flattered either by the submission of those who court his kindness, or the notice of those who suffer him to court theirs. A head thus prepared for the reception of false opinions, and the projection of vain designs, they easily fill with idle notions, till in time they make their plaything an author: their first diversion commonly begins with an Ode or an epistle, then rises perhaps to a political irony, and is at last brought to its height, by a treatise of philosophy.... The author feels no pain, but while they are wondering at the extravagance of his opinion, and pointing him out to one another as a new example of human folly, he is enjoying his own applause, and that of his companions, and perhaps is elevated with the hope of standing at the head of a new sect.[12]

Johnson's attack was not only personal but political. The *Literary Magazine*, in spite of its name, was at that time a decidedly anti-Newcastle organ, and Johnson well knew Jenyns's intimate connection with the Newcastle administration. He not only disapproved of Newcastle but of Pitt the expansionist, and his contributions exhibit a clear and emphatic set of opinions, anticommercialist, anti-imperialist and anti-expansionist, in the Tory tradition.[13] When Newcastle and Pitt eventually reconciled their differences in the coalition that conducted Britain through the Seven Years' War, the *Literary Magazine* lost its critical spirit and waxed violently patriotic. In November 1756, Johnson ceased to be a regular contributor, and except for stray pieces on Hanway and Jenyns seems to have contributed nothing else. Nevertheless, he made the most of this parting task. Jenyns, who by inclination shrank from open confrontation, could not reply effectively to invective, and Johnson rested in the satisfaction that he had exposed the pretensions of a would-be philosopher handicapped for this particular subject by his class. When, in later years, Boswell thought he recognized an attempt to ridicule Johnson in Bicknell's *Musical Travels in England*, ascribed at that time to Jenyns, Johnson was surprised: "'Ha! (said Johnson) I though I had given *him* enough of it.'"[14]

In spite of the public humiliation, Jenyns refused to be dislodged from his position. The *Free Inquiry* continued on through several subsequent editions in short order and in 1791 came out in France as *Essai sur la Nécessité du Mal*—a more precise title. As late as 1774, Edward Wortley Montague was requesting a copy from Venice, and there were those like the writer in the *Critical Review* who considered it to be a performance of "distinguished merit" and the work of an "able and judicious" writer.[15] When Adam Smith published his first book, *The Theory of Moral Sentiments* (1759), his friend David Hume passed around copies to "such of our acquaintances we thought good judges," individuals who would spread its reputation, including Lord Lyttelton, Walpole, Jenyns, and Burke, and he seemed pleased that Jenyns spoke highly of it.[16] Jenyns himself attempted to answer his detractors in a feeble preface to the edition of 1761, a defence of the work against "all the senseless misapprehensions, and malicious misconstructions, with which it has been tortured"; but this was simply a restatement of his original arguments, exhibiting the disappointment of an honest and well-meaning man who felt he had been misunderstood.

Political Pamphleteer

Having now demonstrated his ability as a prose stylist, Jenyns confidently employed his pen in the discussion of more pressing issues, entering the debate on the second

Militia Bill with his first political pamphlet in 1757. That year, in spite of Newcastle's European alliances, the Seven Years' War began with a series of reversals for British troops, and when the French threatened to invade, the ministry was thrown into a panic over the defenselessness of the country. Pitt now had a bill establishing a national militia passed in the Commons, but Hardwicke blocked it in the Lords. Though troops from Hesse and Hanover, the king's other domains, had been hired to guard British soil, when Pitt came to power in 1757 he resolved to make clear demands upon the patriotism of the British people: the Hessians and Hanoverians returned to Germany and the debate on the Militia Bill resumed. While the debate was progressing at Westminster, Jenyns produced a characteristically ironic pamphlet entitled *Short But Serious Reasons for a National Militia*, beginning straightfaced, "In this age of levity and ridicule, it is extremely difficult to procure a serious attention to any proposal, however important, or however wisely calculated for the public benefit. . . ." From there he proceeded to engage in levity and ridicule of his own with five absurd "recommendations" that are no recommendations at all. This piece of political jobbery did not help Hardwicke's cause, and it was quickly swallowed up in a surge of patriotism inspired by Pitt. Once again, its author felt the sting of a counterattack, this time from a pamphlet defending the bill and marveling that the country could possess a spirit who, in a moment of national crisis, could address the public "in a Strain as mortal-merry as the Grave-diggers in *Hamlet*, throwing about their Wit amidst grinning skulls. . . ."[17] Jenyns's facetiousness failed in the end to assist Newcastle and Hardwick. In June the Militia Bill received the endorsement of the Lords and the matter ended. The pamphlet was an ill-conceived endeavor, but it had introduced Jenyns to another role in political life.

Before the next pamphlet appeared, events threatened the security of his seat in the House of Commons once again. Though Jenyns's interests lay in Cambridgeshire, since 1754 he had actually been sitting for Dunwich under the patronage of Sir Jacob Downing, according to the conditions of an intricate arrangement worked out by Lord Hardwicke.

Downing now claimed that he was owed a peerage for his part in that arrangement, but since no peerage had yet been offered him, he decided to go into opposition and announced he would never again support Jenyns's reelection while Jenyns was Newcastle's nominee. This change of events left Jenyns dangling awkwardly in between, for although he was not legally bound to retire, convention demanded that a member surrender his seat when a dispute arose with his patron. Now, both his patrons were at odds with one another.

Hardwicke attempted to intercede, explaining that Jenyns had been seated as a favor to *him* and not to Newcastle; but Downing rejected this construction, and when Jenyns returned to Bottisham that summer, he had no prospect of returning to Parliament. Luckily, in July, the Cambridge M.P. Viscount Dupplin was elevated to the peerage on the death of his father, Lord Kinnoul, and when Hardwicke raised no objection, he recommended that Jenyns replace him. "I do not know any Gentleman of the Neighbourhood who can be prepared, in which all ye others will acquiesce except Mr. Jenyns," he wrote.[18] Though it was not quite so easy to get elected in the town of Cambridge as it had been to represent the rotten borough of Dunwich, as he would soon see, Jenyns eagerly agreed to run when he heard that Newcastle thought him the best choice to establish the Whig interest there and that Hardwicke would assist with election expenses. Accordingly, he was returned once again, this time as the representative of a town in which voting was superintended by a corporation, an oligarchical body of about 150 men dominated by neighboring landowners. His success significantly marked the expansion of the Yorke influence in Cambridge, where it triumphed again in the election of 1761, returning Jenyns and Charles Sloane Cadogan unopposed.

The accession of George III in 1760 inaugurated a new phase of British politics in which existing political structures fell away and the administration of government passed from the hands of one royal favorite to another. George II had previously employed the great Whig families for government administration and delegated to them the dispensing of the immense patronage of the crown, breeding in Parliament a vast array of placemen like Jenyns himself; but with the arrival of George III, the earl of Bute assumed authority over Pitt and Newcastle. Newcastle's great network of patronage stood useless, and in the ensuing years, men like Jenyns changed their attachments more than once in order to keep their places. After Bute had presided over the end of the Seven Years' War and then resigned over the introduction of a tax on cider, the king arranged a ministry under George Grenville, who with the war behind him attempted to lighten taxation and deflate the national debt, both measures being borne principally by the country gentry, who were spending more than 15 percent of their incomes on taxes. Was it not logical, Grenville argued, that the Americans, now relieved of the French menace, should share the cost? In 1765, the government accordingly placed a stamp duty on legal transactions in America, the proceeds to be used for the cost of colonial defense; but the Americans viewed the move as an act of tyranny and rose up in revolt. They would pay no taxes without representation in Parliament. Over the issue of American representation, Jenyns entered a fierce pamphlet debate.

The question at issue was whether colonists had a right to be taxed without being represented directly at Westminster. The act's defenders asserted that even though no colonial members sat in Parliament, the colonists were "virtually" represented like the many Englishmen who lacked direct representation. This was the position adopted by Jenyns, who entered the controversy early with a pamphlet bringing to bear his deft turn of phrase and the prejudices of one who had sat for so long at a forum such as the Board of Trade. Full of confidence tinged with arrogance, he first questioned why any defense of the act should be necessary at all since the protests of the colonists were absurd, "mixt up with several patriotic and favourite words, such as Liberty, Property, Englishmen, &c," reformist language he abhorred. On the subject of consent, he reduced the problem to three spurious propositions: that no Englishman can be taxed without his own consent, without the consent of those he chooses to represent him, or without the consent of a majority "elected by himself and others of his fellow-subjects to represent him." On this last proposition he rested his argument, pointing out that because so few Englishmen could qualify to vote at that time, not all *Englishmen* voted and not all large centers of population even possessed their own members. This, of course, was the very source of American unrest, and when Jenyns drew the last proposition to a startlingly ridiculous extreme ("Why does not this imaginary representation extend to America, as well as over the whole island of Great Britain?"), he left himself vulnerable. By offering the standard conservative argument for virtual representation, Jenyns argued in a circle and did so in a patronizing tone that underestimated the Americans' skill and determination. Their replies soon issued forth.

The two pamphlets bearing most directly on this declaration came from two American lawyers, Daniel Dulany and James Otis.[19] Dulany was one of the most politically competent men in America. The son of a wealthy Maryland official, he had been educated at Eton, Clare College, and the Temple and was thoroughly experienced in legal argumentation. His pamphlet was a thorough statement of the colonists' position, and it attracted many readers in America in spite of its encrustation of legalisms and tangled clauses, perhaps because it dealt not only with the matter of representation but also with the related matter of the trade relationship between Britain and the colonies. And though in the end it diverted to a rambling tour through the author's trade theories, it came swiftly to the point in the opening pages, declaring that since "virtual representation" was the principle on which turned the rectitude of the tax, something more tangible than the mere expression of that principle was needed. In Britain, it continued, nonelectors at least felt represented because they shared the interests and causes of those who *did* cast votes.[20]

At the same time as this, Otis's *Considerations on Behalf of the Colonists*, while it maintained the same political line of argument, personally attacked Jenyns himself. A Harvard law graduate and a man of letters in his own right, Otis possessed the ability to match Jenyns's derisive wit, and he did so, describing Jenyns's carefully measured prose as "a curious specimen of his talent at chicanery and quibbling." He was familiar, he said, with the patronage system in Britain from which placemen like Jenyns had sprung and questioned the implicit faith of a "ministerial mercenary pamphleteer" in a completely authoritarian method of election. Otis shared Dulany's view that the nonvoting classes in Britain still enjoyed representation because they shared common interests with the voters and could at least make their voices heard. If one were to accept Jenyns's argument that the citizens of Manchester, Birmingham, and Sheffield also received no representation, he said, one could just as easily demonstrate that the British House of Commons represented "all the people of the globe" as those in America.[21] Finally, perhaps the clearest analysis of Jenyns's logic, a pamphlet probably written by John Fothergill,[22] showed that Jenyns was to be read circumspectly because he was arguing from precedent and not from principle. "The public," it said, "especially the Americans, expected arguments from this performance, but they are treated with sarcasms; 'They looked for bread, and behold a stone.'"[23]

Jenyns weathered this debate, and the government itself repealed the Stamp Act before the end of 1765. Nevertheless, the pamphlet probably saved Jenyns his position at the Board of Trade. That same year, the king's uncle, the duke of Cumberland, briefly rose to prominence during one of the king's fits of madness and, indeed, would have remained in control as regent had the monarch not recovered. In the interim, Cumberland began to negotiate the formation of a new ministry, and Soame Jenyns suddenly ranked with "Persons, That may be removd" from the Board of Trade. Even when the king rallied to establish yet another administration under the marquess of Rockingham, his name continued to stand among those threatened with the loss of their places.[24] By July, Grenville speculated that he did not know "whom else they mean to proscribe or whom else to reward for the merit or demerit which they have had to him," though he was assured "all the Board of Trade except Mr. Eliot, Mr. Rice, and Mr. Jenyns are in the number of the former. . . ."[25] Jenyns now had no patron. Lord Hardwicke was dead. Yet he voted with Rockingham and survived, clinging to his place at the board until Rockingham himself resigned in 1766.

Jenyns's third pamphlet appeared the following year. With the return of Pitt, those who had previously supported Newcastle renewed their attacks, focusing particularly on the immense national debt and the inflation lingering after the end of the Seven Years' War. Jenyns's pamphlet, *Thoughts on the Causes and Consequences of the Present High Price of Provisions*, was not an attack on government but a discourse on economics in clear, direct prose untouched with irony and lacking his characteristic shafts of wit. As a statement of the conservative view of economics, it was one of his most competent essays. Jenyns reduced the cause of inflation in this instance to two sources: the increase in the national debt and what he called "public poverty and private opulence," the disparity existing between the state of the economy and the standard of living, the "fatal disease" that has destroyed empires. As he went on to explain, the increase of the money supply encourages consumption, so that "Twenty rich families will consume ten times as much meat, bread, butter, soap, and candles, as twenty poor families consisting of the same number; and the prices of all these must certainly rise in proportion to the demand" (2:172–73). Provisions were not dearer, he argued; money was cheaper. To offset these effects, the remedies he was advancing were sound measures for dealing with an inflationary economy: pay off the national debt, shut off opportunities for commerce at the public expense, put an end to colonial settlement based on parliamentary estimates, and avoid new wars. It was a confident statement by an experienced, pragmatic parliamentarian, and it conveyed a sound knowledge of the effects of government finance. But Jenyns was not one of those likely to suffer from the measures he was recommending. He was writing from a privileged point of view, and his critics quickly noticed the limitations placed upon his view by his social position.

The first to take issue was an anonymous and facetious gentleman in Jenyns's own constituency whom William Cole identified as the Reverend Samuel Peck, fellow of Trinity College and vicar of Trumpington.[26] Avoiding the substance of Jenyns's brief, Peck blamed court dependents for raising the expense of government, singling out Jenyns as a placeman whose pension added to that cost, a substantial landowner who would never feel the effects of restraint. He concluded on a threatening note: "You will, however, I suppose, still continue to receive your allowance of a thousand pounds a year for doing—nothing. And, indeed, Sir you had best continue to receive it; for, if I am not greatly mistaken, you will have occasion for that, and all the other sums you can collect, against the ensuing general election. The price of votes, you observe (and I dare say you speak from experience) is, like that of all other commodities, advanced. . . ."[27]

This was not nearly so acrimonious and deflating as the postscript to a pamphlet by George Lowe, also printed that year. Lowe had studied the economic difficulties more thoroughly than Peck and thought he had detected Jenyns's usual ironic tone. He was replying, he said, "lest ridicule should be mistaken for reasoning, or misrepresentation for truth. . . ." Lowe charged Jenyns with applying "court sophistry" to a complicated problem and with writing "more like a wit than a philosopher," aiming "rather to laugh than to reason men out of their opinions." He offered the view that bounties on exported commodities had created artificially high prices at home, thus bringing about a decrease in manufacturing, a decline in trade, and general hardship. He reserved his strongest words for country gentlemen like Jenyns, who maintained country residences while living in town in "luxury and extravagance," wasting their wealth and "hanging their offspring on their country for support."[28] Jenyns's constant attachment to the faction in power left him vulnerable to these kinds of rebukes: no matter how useful his own insights, critics preferred to paint him as a spokesman of the government or the landed interest. This particular exchange was not so much a discusssion of economics as of class differences. It was but one manifestation of a radical reform movement gathering force in Britain.

Jenyns sought reelection for the first time since Hardwicke's death in the election of 1768, and with the support of the Whig organization, he as well as Cadogan held his seat unopposed. With these repeated and easy victories, the two now began to neglect the voters: no longer did they offer their constituents the customary attention, no longer did they render the customary financial "assistance" to individuals, and after the election, people voiced their dissatisfaction with both the members and Lord Montfort, their manager. They felt manipulated for political expediency. Like so many other eighteenth-century politicians, Jenyns and Cadogan adapted their policies to successive ministries and as placemen retained their appointments in all conscience through the minister in power. Jenyns stayed at the Board of Trade from 1755 until he retired; Cadogan, over the same period, was keeper of the Privy Purse to the prince of Wales, surveyor of the King's Gardens, and master of the mint. The changes of allegiance required to maintain such a standing now aroused a minority of the Corporation of Cambridge who had decided to oppose North. Their leader was William Weales, a former mayor, and their slogan was "Wilkes and liberty."[29] Radicalism had arrived in Cambridgeshire and would make its presence felt at the next election.

Throughout the 1770s, Lord North clung to power as first lord of the Treasury in spite of the growth of the parliamentary reform movement and the traumatic breach between Britain and the American colonies. Within Parliament, he managed to reconcile the factions that had attached themselves to his predecessors, Grenville, Rockingham, Chatham, and Grafton, and by so doing satisfied both the Commons and the king. As Burke put it in *Thoughts on the Cause of the Present Discontents* (1770), politics was a combination of personalities, prejudices, and local affiliations instead of a system of intellectually grounded principles or of party loyalty. Unlike their modern counterparts, those in power did not govern from a set of political principles in the modern sense but concerned themselves with administering the judicial and executive machinery of state. About one third of the members of Parliament were courtiers, placemen like Jenyns himself or secretaries who looked to the king for permanence, in return supporting the minister the king chose as leader. Immune from the instability of the changing leadership, the "Court Cabal" (as Burke called them) provided a kind of continuity. As one of these courtiers, Jenyns recognized that the role of government lay in the maintenance of law and order and the provision of financial support for British military and colonial commitments around the world.

In the midst of this changing political pattern, Jenyns wrote his next pamphlet, an ironic performance called *A Scheme for the Coalition of Parties* (1772), a "plain and simple scheme" to save Parliament the time and energy committed to fashioning new ministries, all the more wasteful because there seemed to be no obvious differences of principle among the factions involved. To put an end to such contests for power and profit, he proposed an "annual administration" of both houses of Parliament contrived by lottery so as to end all contests and the corruption that follows them. This scheme was designed to destroy all opposition in Parliament. In case readers were alarmed by that prospect, Jenyns assured them that it would still continue among the people: "it will remain in the hearts and mouths of common-councilmen, liverymen, and freeholders, to watch over the conduct of ministers . . ." (2:270–71). Only in closing did Jenyns refer to the true target of his pamphlet, the radicals of the parliamentary reform movement, especially the Society of Supporters of the Bill of Rights, formed in 1769 during the Wilkes affair. "And here, by the bye," he wrote, "I cannot but applaud the honest sagacity of that honourable society, the Supporters of the Bill of Rights, who have declared eternal war with all great men, esteeming them dangerous coadjutors in the cause of liberty, and wisely concluding, that it is impossible that persons possessed of exalted titles, vast property, and extensive power, should ever be in earnest, in endeavouring to destroy their own superiority, and the subordination of others" (2:271–72). This time, Jenyns did not simply rely upon his irony to be self-evident. He went so far as to caution the reader that "not any wit, nor any humour" was intended. Were it not clear to all that Jenyns was a constitutionalist rather than a party man, it would be tempting to interpret *A Scheme for the Coalition of Parties* as a liberal document. A glance at Jenyns's other political writings, however, would have shown that that was not the case. For the moment, the pamphlet did not raise a response even though it established his attitude toward radicalism.

Placeman and Metaphysician

Jenyns did not produce another pamphlet until after he retired from public life in 1780, and in the meantime he did not speak out on a political issue except for another well-publicized piece of light verse appearing in various newspapers as the American colonies were about to declare their independence in 1775. That year, after General Howe had lost half his force at the battle of Bunker Hill, George Washington took charge as commander in chief of the American army. The cabinet prepared for war, faced with the dilemma of giving up the American colonies or attempting the expensive and repugnant task of conquering them by force of arms.

One thinker who openly advocated a breach with the American colonies was the dean of Gloucester, Josiah Tucker, one of Britain's most formidable political polemicists and one of the first to envisage the whole range of economics as a subject worthy of scientific enquiry. Tucker had been predicting for ten years that the Americans were aiming at independence. Instead of fighting a prolonged war, he had favored expulsion of the American colonies from the empire, demonstrated the futility of attempting to enforce the Stamp Act, and predicted that Britain would retain colonial trade in the long run while escaping the usual expenses of protection and bounties. In a few years, he argued, these same colonies would be back petitioning for reunion. Like the classical economists of a later time, Tucker regarded self-interest as the psychological basis of economics, and long before the revolt in America he had declared that only self-interest bound the colonies to the mother country. In 1775, when these same colonies were all but lost, Tucker proposed an act of Parliament to proclaim them "totally cut off, severed, and separated from the British Empire," leaving them unprotected and anxious to return in a few years to look for support in the struggle against the French and the Indians.[30]

At that point, Jenyns had not made up his mind how the Americans should be handled, and he had told Philip Yorke (who had succeeded his father as Lord Hardwicke), "There seems to be no Medium now between conquering America & giving it quite up, the first I am afraid is impracticable & the other no-body can do."[31] Tucker's plan appealed to him, and after a bluestocking assembly in London he wrote a burlesque ballad that Mrs. Boscawen claimed she herself inspired. "He and I were talking of Dr. Tucker's last pamphlet, and of his plan to cast off ye Americans," she wrote. "Mr. Jenyns said he was a proselite to it, and I answer'd that it seem'd to resemble a piece of mechanism I had heard of, introduc'd in the make of a carriage, that if y^r horses are unruly and kick, you may by means of a spring pull up a peg or plug, and off goes the fore-carriage, horses, and all."[32] Soon the verses came back and made their way around the bluestocking circle before eventually appearing that same year in the *London Chronicle* and then subsequently in the *St. James's Chronicle*, the *Scots Magazine*, the *Gentleman's Magazine*, and the *Annual Register* with such titles as "America," "The Pin," and "The American Coachman." Again, Jenyns indulged his taste for burlesque in this animal fable set in the form of a ballad. First he praised the inventor of the carriage pin, the attachment that allowed a driver to set free his horses if he lost control. But soon the interest shifted to the horses themselves, who were running off at full speed with no sense of direction. The poem concluded,

>Hungry at last, and blind, and lame,
> Bleeding at nose and eyes;
>By sufferings growing mighty tame,
> And by experience wise;
>
>With bellies full of liberty,
> But void of oats and hay;
>They both sneak back, their folly see,
> And run no more away.
>
>Let all who view th' instructive scene,
> And patronize the plan,
>Give thanks to Gloucester's honest Dean,
> For, Tucker,—thou'rt the man.
>   (1:205)

It was a characteristically clever piece of versifying, and it received a great deal of attention in the press in the year of American independence, particularly from radicals and American sympathizers.

Placeman and Metaphysician

Jenyns's views on reform in Britain itself found their clearest expression in his last pamphlet, *Thoughts on a Parliamentary Reform* (1784), a serious and thoughtful defense of the status quo. Popularized by Wilkes and championed in the Commons by Burke, the struggle for reform in Parliament culminated in the measures introduced by the younger Pitt after the election of 1784. Prior to that, the reformers had been pressing for three basic changes: one-year parliaments, the secret ballot, and universal suffrage—all of which Jenyns opposed because he found them impracticable. In particular, he expressed his horror at the prospect of "multitudes of all descriptions and denominations" going out to vote without any method of registration in the country. It would be difficult, he said, to imagine men of property and power enjoying the same share of influence in the legislature as "every pauper, gypsy, vagrant, and least of all every poacher." Moreover, he also raised his voice against the clamor for greater independence in Parliament, which would allow a majority of the members to oppose any administration, the concept of a majority "party" not being a feature of parliamentary government at that time. Under such a system, he warned, no business would ever be transacted, for men act entirely out of self-interest, and once it is removed they have "no star to steer by." An independent House of Commons, he concluded, was "no part of the English constitution" since the constitution provided for three powers. If one became independent, it would change the form of government itself. The philosophical advantages of such a change could not yet be foreseen.

The reviewers once again focused on the tone of these remarks as much as their substance, particularly on Jenyns's condescension. The *Monthly Review* concluded that "his talents for declamation and ridicule seem to be superior to his powers of argumentation," and the *European Magazine*, in a particularly truculent mood, observed, "This ingenious and well-known Sophist . . . has here amused the public with a specimen of his politicks, written in the usual spirit of Hocus Pocus." His performance, it said, was to be considered "as mere matter of entertainment; being no more than a string of pleasantries, calculated to shew off his ironical powers in reconciling contradictory principles, or seeming to reconcile them."[33] Likewise, the radicals quickly buried their enemy under an avalanche of *ad hominem* rebuttals written in the same mocking spirit as the original. One writer charged that Jenyns had "wantonly designed, by the shafts of ridicule, to add to the wounds of a bleeding constitution."[34] Another, more forceful and spirited in his language, seized upon Jenyns's condescension as an excuse for a personal insult. He abhorred, he said, men who are "neither ashamed, nor afraid, to prostitute their splendid abilities to the diabolical purposes of rivetting upon their country the general chains of venality and corruption; who dare to bid a nation despair of all integrity and virtue in its Legislature for ever; and set themselves maliciously to mock at the very little virtue they cannot reason out of the world." And seizing upon Jenyns's phrase that "in the language of the times" an independent Parliament would hamper any administration, he added, "whether it were vogue to speak Court or Country, Whig or Tory, the Honourable Gentleman always spoke the language of the present times."[35]

The most vigorous reply issued from Major John Cartwright, a reformer who had already published an impressive list of reform documents but whose extreme views had made him unacceptable to the Whigs. In a long pamphlet, typically dry and earnest, he set out to show with reference to Jenyns's book *A View of the Internal Evidence of the Christian Religion* (1776) how the Tory opposition to the movement was inconsistent with Christianity. Jenyns, he said, was hoping to stem the tide of truth and give novelty to his subject at the same time: in his dilemma, he had turned to wit and ridicule "as a last resource." Cartwright's prose brought out the full force of his radical fervor, and the result was some of the strongest language Jenyns had ever seen used against him. Cartwright called Jenyns's composition "a sin of silly vanity, classic pride, and literary buffoonery; proceeding from a mind in which knowledge and ignorance, politeness and vulgarity, refinement and grossness, wit and stupidity, sense and absurdity, right and wrong, morality and impiety, religion and profligacy, have been strangely mixed and jumbled together, and floating at random in a perpetual chaos."[36] After this assault, Jenyns never ventured an opinion on political matters again. He did prepare one other pamphlet, "Thoughts on the National Debt" (2:275–304), a document covering much of the same ground as the one on the high price of provisions, but it was never sent to the printer.

The Election of 1774

During the 1760s, Soame Jenyns emerged from the shadow of Lord Hardwicke and established himself as a more independent figure. He knew the most important political and literary luminaries in the country, and as a result his interest shifted from Cambridgeshire to London. In 1761, we find him joining the Society for the Encouragement of Arts, Manufacturers and Commerce, one of the societies founded at mid-century to study progress in trade, commerce, and the industrial arts. In the days when technology was not a specialized field of study, this society attracted men of widely divergent interests—Dr. Charles Burney, Sir Joseph Banks, Johnson, Boswell, Garrick, Reynolds, and Horace Walpole, to name only a few. We also find Jenyns more and more in the company of the "bluestocking" group, the circle of intellectual women who substituted books for cards. At Bath, he and his devoted wife mixed with the social elite during their regular migrations, stopping to visit local landowners as they progressed there.[37] On one such visit in 1769, he "sat half an hour" with Lord Chesterfield. In 1771 he entertained at Bottisham Joseph Banks and his colleague Charles Clarke, who had just returned from the *Endeavour* expedition, and received a report of their findings.[38] By the end of the decade he seems to have taken his social position and his constituents for granted, so that when the time came to face the voters again, he found politics in the town of Cambridge greatly altered.

At the venerable age of seventy, Jenyns passed one of the most unpleasant interludes of his life during the election of 1774, a contest in which he first encountered the interference of radicals in the electoral system. Since it was no longer possible to rely on patronage for votes in Cambridge, for the first time in twenty-five years the squire of Bottisham faced hostile opposition and experienced the brutal realities of mob violence. From the last election, Jenyns and Cadogan had maintained their respective sinecures but neglected the voters. Now, they found, this had been a serious mistake. In those days, members of Parliament were expected not only to attend to the needs of their constituents but, in the absence of government services, to contribute generously to local projects. "What added to the Opposition," wrote the Reverend William Cole, "was the little Attention paid by the old members to their Constituents, & the great Parsimony & Niggardliness of both."[39] Though no election had been contested in the town since 1737, a group opposed to the incumbents now formed under the leadership of William Weales, a former mayor. While Weales could not claim many supporters within the corporation itself, he stirred up plenty of popular enthusiasm outside the electorate with the undoubted encouragement of the Manners family, who consistently voted against the government and found their influence expanding in the county after 1760, following the death of Lord Hardwicke. Two opposition candidates now appeared—Thomas Plumer Byde, a Hertfordshire gentleman, and Samuel Meeke, a timber merchant from Lambeth—and by September they had begun to canvass actively.

Realizing the threat of defeat for the first time, the incumbents bestirred themselves. During what Jenyns called "the most disagreeable & fatiguing week I ever pass'd," they visited the homes of freemen, called at the colleges, and rode about the county giving dinners and soliciting votes, all the activity appearing futile when their opponents ceremoniously arrived in town with a mounted escort and band and proceeded to Trumpington, where a large crowd unharnessed their horses and drew their carriage to the White Bear Inn for an election dinner.[40] Similar scenes could be observed over the next few days. At the time, William Cole assessed the incumbents' chances and made this prediction: "Two people, without ever being heard of three months ago . . . people utterly unknown and unconnected with any of the corporation or county, have been searched out and brought to Cambridge to stir up an opposition. It seems to me as if they would shake the old interest, if not carry the day. . . ."[41] Confident of victory, the challengers appeared on the morning of 8 October wearing orange ribbons in their hats and paraded about the town with a band. When the voters had assembled in the town hall, the drama began.

Despite noisy protestations, a prepared statement was first read soliciting all candidates to sign a declaration calling for the following reforms: (1) the establishment of a fairer and more equal representation of the people in Parliament, (2) greater toleration of Protestant Dissenters, (3) restoration to the Americans of the right of taxation by representation, and (4) the repeal of the Quebec Act, the Boston Port Act, the act altering the constitution of Massachusetts, and the act permitting those accused of offenses in America to be tried in Britain. Candidates were also urged to promote acts to strengthen "the Civil and Religious Liberties of the People," to give "due attendance" in Parliament, and to neither accept nor hold a "place" or "pension." Such open radicalism was an affront to the supporters of Jenyns and Cadogan, but for the moment they were outnumbered and the motion passed.[42] Byde and Meeke signed the declaration. Jenyns and Cadogan refused. Buoyed up with the anticipation of victory, the radicals now called for the vote, and when the count had been taken, the challengers did indeed receive a majority from the freemen of the town. They were defeated ultimately, however, when the gentry and the rest of the aldermen voted together to protect the landed interest.

Election day was far from finished. A "dumb peel" rang out from Great St. Mary's, and a mob erupted into a riot characteristic of radical politics. As the voters emerged from the town hall, it attacked a carriage load of beer drawn up on the market hill to celebrate the victory and proceeded to stave in the vessels, breaking the carriage itself into pieces and starting a bonfire with the wheels and wood. As the winners were about to be chaired about the town, it pelted them with the staves. Alderman Gifford, the corporation's election manager, received injuries that, according to William Cole, caused his death three months later. The supporters of Jenyns and Cadogan dared not venture forth wearing their green and white ribbons, and the victorious incumbents themselves only reached the Rose Tavern to celebrate with the protection of constables. When more beer appeared on the hill, the friends of Byde and Meeke consumed it. "They were so sure of their victory," wrote William Cole, "that the Disappointment was a Mortification they could not support: they were almost stark mad with Vexation: so buoyed up had they been by their foolish Managers."[43] Next, extra constables had to be sworn in to keep the peace, but the mob nevertheless carried on to attack the Rose Inn, where the celebration was in progress, smashing in the windows. Gentlemen were roughly knocked down and detained from venturing home, though they eventually escaped through an exit at the rear. It was midnight before Cambridge returned to its customary academic tranquillity again.

Soame Jenyns, accustomed to the felicities of London life, called it "the most disagreeable Day w[ch] I ever saw." He knew that although he had triumphed, his difficulties with his constituents had only begun. Times had changed since his entry into politics a generation before: people were demanding more of their representatives. Uncomfortable in his dealings with the common man on that basis, he ignored the clamor for reform during the ensuing term. He would not have entered the election at all had he known the consequences, and indeed he had let his name stand only because he could not have honorably let the side down. He had, he confessed, been caught in the unfortunate dilemma of seeking the seat for the Yorke interest as a loyal placeman and later discovering "the Impossibility of laying hold on one moment, when It could have been given up wth honour or even Decency to our Constituents to Government, & one another."[44]

Chapter Three
Apostle to the Dissipated
A "Pretty Book" on the Christian Religion

After the publication of the *Free Inquiry* in 1757 and the odium surrounding it as a result of Johnson's review, Soame Jenyns wrote no philosophical prose for nearly thirty years. In the meantime, he continued to be read and regarded circumspectly as a political and philosophical commentator with a rather ironic, capricious turn of mind, if not as a deist. The term "deist," however, was often used imprecisely in the eighteenth century, particularly as a term of abuse, and there is therefore no reason to suspect that Jenyns ever swerved to unorthodox beliefs. Yet by the time he reached seventy, there had been a great change in English metaphysics: the great arguments of natural religion that had dominated English thought in Jenyns's youth had buckled under the onslaught of Bishop Butler and no longer provided sufficient "evidence," in the empirical sense, for establishing the credibility of Christianity (see chapter 6). Butler's *Analogy of Religion, Natural and Revealed* (1736) had set up a fresh line of defense against rationalists such as the deists by furnishing a new pattern of probabilities for Christian apologists seeking to verify the truth of revelation. And it was as a defender of revelation with a similar purpose that Jenyns returned to philosophical prose in his most widely acclaimed and influential work, *A View of the Internal Evidence of the Christian Religion* (1776), a Christian apology earnest in tone and free of the sophistry and wit of his previous publications. Indeed, the change was surprising. When shown a copy by Boswell, David Hume remarked, "I am told there is nothing of his usual spirit in it."[1] Clearly, it was more direct and sincere than usual, couched in the language of piety and aimed at "busy and idle persons" so engrossed in the pursuits of this world that they had not the leisure to learn from the weightier discourses already available.

In publishing this volume, Jenyns thus associated himself with the innovating apologists of the later eighteenth century who accentuated the moral qualities of the Christian religion as an argument for its validity rather than the standard defensive arguments from prophecy and miracle. For while these apologists shared with the deists a belief in God, virtue, and immortality, they also believed that these were known supremely in the events surrounding the life of Christ, effecting a transition from a rationalistic to a moral conception of religion. Rationalist theology had attempted to answer the challenge of the New Science. Whether one was interpreted in the light of the other or whether clear distinctions were made between the two, the implications of science for theology had had to be faced. But for these later apologists, no such conflict could arise. They defined Christianity as a moral realm existing side by side with science and independent of it.

Jenyns's treatise, then, is a restatement of the familiar argument that the divine origin of Christianity may be inferred from the purity and originality of its ethics, and as such it exaggerates the contrast between Christian and pagan morality often put forward by deistic writers. Virtues characteristic of the pagan world, such as valor, patriotism, and friendship, says Jenyns, have "no intrinsic merit" in them. Valor is merely "constitutional," or endowed, and patriotism and friendship fall short of the general benevolence of Christianity because we bestow them upon particular objects. The characteristically Christian virtues of forgiveness, charity, repentance, faith, and humility are superior to these because instead of adapting to the world, they improve it wherever they are accepted. Even if they are not accepted, they are intrinsically superior to the preoccupations of the world, and this is the proof of their divine origin. The great design of Christianity is to "enlighten the minds, purify the religion, and amend the morals" of mankind and to "select" the meritorious to be "successively transplanted" into the kingdom of heaven. On the basis of this line of argument, Jenyns proceeds to minimize the importance of external evidences such as prophecy and miracle and to suggest that the Scriptures are not revelations from God but the *history* of such revelations.

Such a reassuringly moral yet intellectual interpretation of the value of Christianity was quite welcome at a time when traditional values seemed to be giving way to scientific enquiry and skepticism, and as a result, no publication of Jenyns's received such an enthusiastic response. "Few publications, on their first appearance, have been more generally read . . ." wrote John Nichols, the bookseller.[2] Within a month of its publication, Dodsley purchased the copyright for two hundred and fifty pounds.[3] In 1776 alone it sold five editions in Britain while others were appearing in Ireland and also in America, where Patrick Henry had it printed "for popular use" at his own expense during his second term as governor of Virginia (1790) and distributed it to young men influenced by fashionable French skepticism.[4] Outside the English-speaking world, there were translations in French, Polish, and modern Greek. Jenyns's sincerity and clarity made the book attractive to readers of a whole range of belief. Charles Nalson Cole, Jenyns's editor, claims that while he was going through Jenyns's papers he encountered testimonials to its inspirational value, acknowledgments testifying that it had led readers "from unbelief to a full conviction of the truths he had endeavoured to establish," including one from India estimating that Jenyns's propositions proved "all that is wanted to be cleared up."[5] Hester Thrale, the intimate of Johnson, liked to tell the story of the young man resolved to enter Holy Orders who explained, upon being examined by the bishop about his reading, that he had made up his mind only recently and had not had much time for it: "well Sir cries the Bishop what *have* you read? why my Lord returns the Youth, I have read Mr Soame Jennings's Book, that I have—*quite through.*"[6]

While the book brought satisfaction and understanding to the common reader, it also attracted the attention of both the clergy and the literary and political luminaries of London. Soon after its publication, Thomas Hutchinson, the former governor of Massachusetts, wrote in his diary, "In the evening at Dr Heberden's. Soame Jenyns's book upon the internal evidence of the Christian Religion much applauded."[7] The Reverend Thomas Scott, later to be the author of *The Force of Truth* (1779), read it after a fellow clergyman had recommended it in a visitation sermon, receiving from it "more distinct heart-affecting views of the design of God in this revelation of himself" than he had before; and Boswell, who stayed home one afternoon to read it, found himself pleased with the "ease" with which the subject was handled, the "gentlemanly style," and the absence of divine precepts about sexual intercourse.[8] The poet and philosopher James Beattie, writing to Sir William Forbes (later bishop of Worcester), acknowledged that the book was one of Forbes's favorites and that he himself thought Jenyns had done his argument "more justice than any other author I am acquainted with." Beattie had planned such a treatise himself, it seems, so as to make the subject "plain and entertaining, and suited to all capacities, especially to those of young people," but recognized that Jenyns's had preempted it.[9] And the Reverend William Jones of Nayland revealed how he had received an enquiry about it while on a tour of the Continent from someone who had heard about it in Brussels. "To say the truth," he said, "I should have been ashamed of myself, if I had been found ignorant of that book when I was questioned about it at *Paris*. . . . "[10] It was still being read by undergraduates at Cambridge in the early nineteenth century.

Other readers, however, were not so ready to approve as to turn the book into a subject of controversy. There were those suspicious of the author's apparent shift from the less orthodox *Free Inquiry*; others thought they detected yet another ironic performance of the kind Jenyns usually applied to political issues; still others could not be sure whether Jenyns faithfully represented the orthodox teachings of the church. "Pray was not his *Origin of Evil* a little heterodox?" Walpole asked the Reverend William Mason. "I have dipped a little into this new piece, and thought I saw something like irony, but to be sure I am wrong, for the *ecclesiastical court* are quite satisfied."[11] Mrs. Elizabeth Carter, the bluestocking, believed Jenyns was sincere but reported there was "a pretty prevailing notion or affectation of a notion" that he was not in earnest; and Edmond Malone, who had often observed Jenyns performing in parliamentary circles, remembered how at that time his best friends were at a loss to know whether it was "serious or comical."[12] Indeed, it was a good deal lighter than most other books of theology, but as Boswell pointed out, that feature made it appealing to most of its readers. When other members of Johnson's circle openly ridiculed this apparently sudden excursion into theology, Boswell defended it, particularly on one occasion when Johnson pronounced

"I think it a pretty book; not very theological indeed; and there seems to be an affectation of ease and carelessness, as if it were not suitable to his character to be very serious about the matter." BOSWELL. "He may have intended this to introduce his book the better among genteel people, who might be unwilling to read too grave a treatise. There is a general levity in the age. We have physicians now with bagwigs; may we not have airy divines, at least somewhat less solemn in their appearance than they used to be?" JOHNSON. "Jenyns might mean as you say."[13]

Undoubtedly, Jenyns's light touch must have misled those accustomed to the gravity of theological writing. Wesley thought he had only "personated" a Christian. "He is undoubtedly a fine writer;" he said, "but whether he is a Christian, Deist, or Atheist, I cannot tell."[14]

In addition to these cursory reactions, more thorough criticism began to trickle from the presses, and by September 1776, the newspapers were soliciting more responses. By the end of the year, so many had been published that they constituted a minor debate destined to endure for the next twelve months before it started to fade. The reviewers received it with applause. The *Gentleman's Magazine* was full of praise, and the *Monthly Review* remained sympathetic even though the book at first excited some "suspicions and apprehensions as to its general tendency," as Abraham Rees wrote. The *Critical Review*, while it took issue with particular points, decided that it could "warmly recommend" the performance to believer and infidel alike.[15] But with the publication of the first pamphlets, Jenyns's intentions began to be questioned. One clergyman who examined the book considered it to be the product of "a man of fashion, retiring to his closet from a dissipated world, to give the momentous points of religion a due examination" and took issue with his interpretations of a future judgment, patriotism, and the payment of taxes. Unable to ignore Jenyns's previous record, he lectured, "A person who sits down to teach others, however he may amuse *himself* with fallacious reasoning, should be exceedingly cautious in what he advances, lest, while he labours to do good, he should be little less destructive to his fellow-creatures."[16] Another Christian author censured him for suggesting that Christianity had been altered, corrupted, and defaced throughout the centuries and appealed for support to the prophecies and declarations of the Old and New Testaments.[17] Jenyns's definition of so-called "Christian" virtues troubled some readers. One objected to the distinction between "active" and "moral" courage and another to the treatment of valor, patriotism, and friendship, the latter charging that Jenyns had treated his subject in an extraordinary manner to attract readers and had perverted the terms in doing so. "For my own part," he said, "being thoroughly convinced of an evil tendency in the passages here considered, I thought it very immaterial whether the composition was merely ironical, or proceeded from the delirium of a superannuated understanding."[18]

In general, these writers refrained from personal insult, being content to defend Christianity where they thought it misrepresented. The only exception was William Kenrick, a hack writer with a jealous, perverse temper and a love of notoriety. Unfortunately, Kenrick took an instant dislike to Jenyns's treatise and attacked him in the pages of the *London Review of English and Foreign Literature*, which he then edited. Both in his own articles and in his replies to correspondents, he acted like a contentious trifler obsessed with the notion that human rationality is insufficient for apprehending religious truth. He then tediously set forth his criticisms in the *London Review* and expanded them into a volume entitled *Observations on Soame Jenyns's View of the Internal Evidence of the Christian Religion; Addressed to its Almost-Christian Author* (1776). One copy he dispatched to the Reverend Samuel Badcock with a profusion of compliments and a request for a review. But when Badcock had examined Kenrick's assaults, he perceived what he called "the speciousness of his *pious* professions" and expressed dissatisfaction with his conclusions. In later years, Badcock explained how he had recognized at once Kenrick's design to bring suspicion on Christianity. "He wished to represent Xtianity as the Religion of Faith & Feeling;" he said, "not of Evidence & Understanding." There is a good chance that Badcock was the author of another publication attempting to reconcile the two antagonists, but in any case no reconciliation took place.[19] Jenyns, as usual, remained silent, and from subsequent numbers of the *London Review* he continued to receive heaps of innuendo and scorn. "It should seem from some of the Answers to that book," wrote the Reverend John Mainwaring, "as if the Author had betrayed, or assaulted the religion he so happily defends."[20] By 1777, only the initial skirmishes had so far taken place. The more considered, scholarly replies resumed the debate without Kenrick's acrimony.

By far the most balanced analysis of *A View of the Internal Evidence of the Christian Religion* was a series of "letters" written by the learned Archibald Maclaine, minister of the English church at The Hague since 1746 and for a time preceptor to the prince of Orange. Like so many other commentators, Maclaine could not be sure whether Jenyns was being serious or not after hearing accounts of his "sly wit" and his "easy and elegant pleasantry." Nevertheless, he maintained a sympathetic tone and presented a thoroughly lucid criticism that was by far the most useful made about the book at that point. He wrote, "One would be tempted sometimes to think, that you, yourself, lost sight of *these* principles in the midst of the desultory detail of arguments and observations, which you bring to support them; and, while we admire several fine touches of genius, wit and eloquence, that strike us in the midst of this splendid confusion, we lament the want of that luminous order and philosophical precision, that are indispensably required in a work of this kind."[21] Maclaine was right. By aiming at a popular readership, Jenyns had not intended to be systematic, and the book's popularity made plain his lack of rigor. Now the scholars began to disagree about the merits of the book as well.

The Reverend Edward Fleet of Oriel College, Oxford, entered the debate with a thorough and spirited refutation of Maclaine, accusing him of mistaking Jenyns's meaning. He could find nothing in the book contrary to the Scriptures, he said, and praised it as a guide to moral behavior and for its tendency to "curb and restrain the licentious prevalency of manners."[22] Maclaine's book was more dangerous in the hands of the idle than Jenyns's, he concluded. The news of this remark and the review of his book in Kenrick's *London Review* infuriated Maclaine, but he refused to be drawn in. Instead, he drafted a reply lacking his usual scholarly style, and his three pages of invective emerged in the *Monthly Review* under the name of Ralph Griffiths, the editor,[23] while Kenrick was also attacking Fleet in the *London Review*. Fleet did attempt a weak defense in *An Address and Reply to the London and Monthly Reviewers* (1777), but it came too late to gain back the advantage.

Not all Jenyns's critics had spoken yet. Two more eminent divines still wished to have their say. Samuel Johnson's companion, Percival Stockdale, fired a passing shot in the introduction to *Six Discourses* (1777), where he judged the book to be a work of "unmerited popularity" brought on by the attentions and congratulations addressed to it by the sovereign. Picking up a common theme, he added that the picture of Christianity drawn by Jenyns had been exhibited from a strain of "egregious folly" or "disingenuous sophistry."[24] A more effective reply was a lengthy treatise in the form of a dialogue written by the Reverend Henry Taylor, the theological writer and wit. Taylor thought he perceived in it a "mischievous" tendency, and one of his characters concluded, "I can't tell what to think of it. I am frequently at a loss to know whether he is writing *for* Christianity or *against* it."[25] Taylor's artful dialogue challenged Jenyns on strictly theological grounds just as rigorously as Maclaine's discourse. By this time, *A View of the Internal Evidence* had been so thoroughly sifted and debated that the more insightful readers hesitated to take the author seriously, particularly in the light of his previous religious views. Jenyns did not help his cause. As usual, he refused to defend himself publicly, and two schools of thought continued to coexist: one praising him for stirring up an interest in living a Christian life and the other condemning him as a wit who would eventually turn men to the devil.

A Collection of Essays

After Soame Jenyns retired from public life, he put together a collection of eight short essays on a variety of philosophical subjects, repeating many of the ideas of his previous works but making no reference to the works themselves or their critics. *Disquisitions on Several Subjects* (1782) reiterated his thoughts on such subjects as the great chain of being, a preexistent state, rational Christianity, government and civil liberty, and other minor concerns, reaffirming without apology his attachment to an established, unreformed system of government and the metaphysics originally expounded in the *Free Inquiry*. Once more, his whimsical and paradoxical language exposed him to criticism, and there were doubts expressed again about the author's apparent return to a more orthodox position a few years before. Critics brought out the familiar sobriquets "sophist" and "wit," accusing Jenyns this time of misrepresenting the religion he had previously claimed to profess. To those readers who could not remember the reception of the *Free Inquiry* twenty-five years before, some of the ideas and the imaginative lengths to which the author was willing to take his empiricism seemed strange indeed.

William Enfield, writing in the *Monthly Review*, described the book as a striking example of how superior abilities may be industriously occupied in erecting "fanciful and paradoxical systems" or in establishing "doctrines inconsistent with the great rights and interests of mankind." The *Critical Review*, while it applauded Jenyns's elegant style, saw in the disquisitions "wild and chimerical notions" and reported that they had failed to satisfy some of those who considered Christianity to be "a rational system" free from absurdities.[26] One of the speculations Jenyns had reiterated was the Platonic theory of a preexistent state, implying that the world was a place of punishment for sins previously committed and that this also accounted for the presence of evil in the world. The *Gentleman's Magazine* thought this system was exposed to "innumerable difficulties," and Horace Walpole, after reading half the book, found himself persuaded that Jenyns was being ironic. Walpole found it difficult to accept the idea that an omnipotent being would inflict punishments without letting the sufferers know about the crimes they had committed. "What discomfort must it be to a poor creature, whose lot is poverty and affliction here," wrote Mrs. Barbauld to Hannah More, "instead of promising himself his portion of good things hereafter, to think that he is only paying off old scores." Caesar Morgan, the Christian apologist, agreed. If the world is to be a place of punishment, he wrote in a detailed, rambling pamphlet, the delinquent should at least be aware that he is suffering for former crimes.[27]

None of these disquisitions stirred up such a response as the seventh, written on the subject of government and civil liberty, a subject of extensive interest during the popular struggle for parliamentary reform. In this essay, Jenyns took issue with the substance of Locke's *Two Treatises of Government* (1690) and by so doing appeared to confirm his opponents' suspicions that he was really a Tory at heart. Following the Revolution, Locke had gained prominence as the chief Whig theorist. His *Two Treatises* stood as an answer to the absolutism of Filmer and Hobbes. Subsequently, his constitutional theories influenced political thinking in both Britain and America. According to Locke, the civil state originated in a "contract" between governor and governed. Though the supreme power rested in the legislative branch of government, he conceded, the governor derived his authority from the consent of the governed, whose welfare he had chosen to seek. This made the task of government a matter of expediency rather than rule. Of the two political groups existing in England since the Revolution, the Whigs reflected this philosophy more closely than the Tories and claimed to be protecting the liberties of the subject; the Tories, on the other hand, professed a devotion to royal prerogative and to the legitimate line of succession to the throne, a line that had been broken in the seventeenth century. In the seventh disquisition, Jenyns appeared to differ with the Whig interpretation by setting out to refute five tenets of Lockean theory: that all men are born equal, that all men are born free, that all government is derived from the people, that all government is a contract between governor and governed, and that no government ought to last if it does not continue to the advantage of the two contracting parties. Because of the strong bias of this essay and because Jenyns's conservatism had so often veered toward the Tory point of view throughout his career, he once again laid himself open to strong criticism.

An answer quickly came from Richard Watson, the bishop of Llandaff and a loyal Whig who was so "vexed" by what he perceived to be Jenyns's Toryism that, though he was ill at the time, he read the book in an afternoon and sent off a response to the *Monthly Review* the next day. Watson thought he had detected an indirect attack on the Whig interest in Parliament and wrote to provide a "feeble antidote" to restore the health of any Whigs who might succumb under the virulence of Jenyns's "poison."[28] The *Monthly Review* also printed long passages of Jenyns's prose, claiming that its sense of public duty compelled it to prevent "the dissemination of absurdity and error, under the sanction of distinguished and respected names."[29] As soon as it appeared, however, another reaction quickly followed from the pen of the Reverend Baptist Noel Turner, a divine who on the contrary thought the book contained a considerable degree of merit. Turner applauded Jenyns's literary skill, and he justifiably praised the disquisition on cruelty to animals, with its catalog of cruelty and horror, as one that was "as worthy of the pen of a Jenyns, as of the pencil of an Hogarth."[30] Turner's particular interest was the disquisition on government, and he went to great lengths to mediate between the two writers, whom he accused of acting partisan. He was especially glad to have an opportunity to refute Locke on this occasion and indeed thought he was making the first regular attack on Locke's "political infallibility" until he found out later that Dean Tucker had already done so the year before.[31]

The one who took the most pleasure from reading the seventh disquisition was Horace Walpole, who had entered Parliament at about the same time as Jenyns and had proceeded to demean him or ridicule his writing at every opportunity. Walpole still resented Jenyns's success as a placeman and seethed over his burlesque poem, *An Ode* (1780), which he took as an attack on Gray. He called the disquisition a "*chef-d'oeuvre* of impudent profligacy" and seized this chance to both embarrass the poet and show the placeman in what he thought to be his true political colors. What followed was an unfortunate example of literary pettiness and political infighting.

First, Walpole urged his cohort William Mason to persuade William Burgh, a writer and former Irish M.P., to publish an answer, and Burgh in fact gave Mason reason to think he would have one before long. Walpole now sat back and rubbed his hands at the prospect. "Whatever happens I shall be overjoyed if Mr Burgh condescends to adopt my idea:" he said, "yet I wish a less vanescent stigma than can be affixed by controversy were imprinted on the old servile buffoon's front. I wish he was beshet."[32] This typically Walpolean vulgarism referred to a private joke shared by the two correspondents after the publication of Mason's *Archaeological Epistle to the Reverend and Worshipful Jeremiah Milles* (1782), one of the satires Mason had written under the pseudonym "Malcolm MacGreggor." Two thirds of the text copied the fake "archaeological" language of the Rowley poems Milles had edited, and the stanza Walpole referred to went as follows:

> So have I seen, in Edinborrowe-towne,
>   A ladie faire in wympled paramente
> Abbrodden goe, whanne on her powrethe downe
>   A mollock hepe, from opper oryal sente;
> Who, whanne shee lookethe on her unswote geare,
> Han liefer ben beshet thann in thilke steynct aumere.[33]

This stanza makes great play with the well-known Edinburgh practice of dumping human waste out the window and into the street. From Mason's "glossary" we learn that the lady was hit by a "moist, or wet heap, or load" poured from an upper window. She announces that she would rather be "beshet" ("shut up") than remain visible in her stained clothing. Walpole, of course, was using the word in quite a different sense. When Burgh failed to produce the expected rebuke, he was forced to wait several weeks more before Mason produced one himself in *The Dean and the 'Squire*, the latest satire in the "Malcolm MacGreggor" series, a rancorous poem directed at Jenyns and Tucker for their political stance.

Previously, Mason had respected Jenyns as a minor versifier. In 1758, when he had sent two of his odes to Gray for inspection, he had predicted confidently that he might "squeeze" himself in on the shelf between Jenyns and Lord Chesterfield. A few years later, he had presented Jenyns with a copy of his elegies and had received in return a polite, decorous reply.[34] In the meantime, Mason had attached himself to the parliamentary reform movement, and with his newly acquired reverence for constitutional liberty he now believed the country was endangered by the very representatives it had elected. He therefore seized upon the recent writings of Jenyns and Tucker on government and civil liberty (written with what he took to be a strong Tory bias) as a good opportunity to attack the Tories, and as soon as he had his *jeu d'esprit* ready for the press, he let Walpole know in advance. "To explain myself concerning my diarrhoea," he wrote. "—You know that lately you wished that somebody was *beshet*; but this was not to be done without *shetting*, and this I have done very plentifully. The *molloch hepe* goes to town with this and will be *sent from opper oryall* very speedily."[35]

When it finally appeared in May 1782, the "eclogue" was a disappointment. The imagined dialogue between the squire and the dean, a "fragment" modeled on Jenyns's own poem, *The 'Squire and the Parson* (1749), had been intended to lampoon Locke's principles of equality and government by consent. However, Mason had strained so eagerly to play the iconoclast that the point got lost among his ponderous Hudibrastics. While an occasional epigram found its mark, the poem as a whole lacked the substance for mounting an attack on a philosophical system. Reduced to personal abuse, Mason could manage only to attack Jenyns himself, particularly in the mock dedication, where he chided him for having served so long as a government pensioner and expressed the wish that "having changed from Tory to Whig in the ministry of the Duke of Newcastle, from Whig to Tory under those, or rather *that* of Lords Bute and North, you may now change again from Tory to Whig under the New Administration...."[36] It was a cheap, ineffectual performance. Walpole applauded it, but over all it disappointed him and he craved a continuation. Mason struggled to comply, and though he resumed the assault when he later responded to Jenyns's *Thoughts on a Parliamentary Reform* (1784) with "The Duchess and Squire, a Political Eclogue on the Subject of a Reform in Parliament," this even more ineffectual performance never reached the hands of the printer.[37] After *The Dean and the 'Squire*, Mason attempted no more satire in collaboration with Walpole, and their friendship ended two years later. As for Jenyns, the verses did him no harm. In 1784 James Barry apotheosized him in a large mural depicting the progress of civilization, placing him among a gathering of distinguished personages that still adorns the walls of the Royal Society of Arts.[38]

A Male Bluestocking

During his last session in Parliament, Soame Jenyns was a busy and animated figure at London social gatherings, and in spite of the animosity he so obviously provoked in some quarters, there is no doubt that his happiest moments were spent not in his cherished Cambridgeshire countryside but in the city where he was born and where he died. His pleasant manner and ease of conversation particularly made him a welcome addition to the evening parties assembled by the intellectual circle of ladies known as the "bluestockings," presided over chiefly by Mrs. Elizabeth Montagu, their acknowledged "queen," for it was she who often selected the appropriate mixture of rank and talent in attendance. The bluestocking gathering was a strange and innovative feature of London life, a mixture of fashionable and political society with a few literary figures who seem to have fitted in comfortably with the arrangement. As Lord Holland recalled, since literary men felt uncomfortable with the effort required to blend with those of business and rank, the literary world was represented by those who encompassed both: men like Horace Walpole, Sheridan, Reynolds, Burke, Lord Bath, Lord Lyttelton, and Jenyns.[39] Nevertheless, one could also find Tickell, Garrick, Gray, Dr. Burney, Boswell, and even Johnson, who disgusted the ladies with his slovenly eating habits and his bullying. Greatness alone did not provide the entrée. Any respectable person likely to contribute to the success of an evening by rank, ability, or powers of conversation received a welcome, and as a result there were some strange groupings indeed. Hannah More commemorated their essence in "Bas Bleu" (1787):

> Here sober Duchesses are seen,
> Chaste Wits, and Critics void of spleen;
> Physicians, fraught with real science,
> And Whigs and Tories in alliance;
> Poets, fulfilling Christian duties,
> Just lawyers, reasonable Beauties;
> Bishops who preach, and Peers who pay,
> And Countesses who seldom play;
> Learn'd Antiquaries, who, from college,
> Reject the rust, and bring the knowledge. . . .[40]

Horace Walpole, a frequenter of such gatherings, conveyed something of their spirit in a report of one meeting at Lady Lucan's in 1781 at which he noticed Mrs. Montagu keeping aloof from the "Demogorgon" Johnson, whose conversational habits she detested. There were also Soame Jenyns, "Persian" Jones, Courtney "the new Court wit," and "the out-pensioners of Parnassus." Of course, beneath the veneer of good will, there were secret enmities and feuds of long standing, and they quickly rose to the surface when boredom set in.[41] Jenyns himself was not one of those ready to make an embarrassing scene in public. With his geniality and wit, he sparkled in his own modest way, and from the beginning of the 1770s he flourished in this environment.

Jenyns endeared himself to the bluestocking ladies because he never offended anyone. Whereas Johnson, by comparison, would not heed an interruption in conversation, Jenyns would put the interrupter right without any slackening of his humor, adding perhaps a preparatory grunt or a few taps on the lid of his snuff box. "He was the man, who bore his part in all societies with the most even temper and undisturbed hilarity of all the good companions, whom I ever knew," recalled Richard Cumberland.[42] Aware of his literary activities, the young and impressionable Hannah More wrote in a similar vein to her family after a *conversazione* at Mrs. Boscawen's to report how Jenyns had gallantly taken her in hand and introduced her to the company. "There is a fine simplicity about him," she said, "and a meek innocent kind of wit, in Addison's manner, which is very pleasant."[43] When Susanna Dobson dedicated her *Life of Petrarch* to him in 1775, she took the trouble to acknowledge in particular the "pleasure" and "improvement" she had received from his conversation. And so we do not hear of him engaging in literary or political disputes in his later years. Instead, he confined his pleasantries to a group that included Richard Owen Cambridge, Richard Cumberland, and Walpole. These three were known as "the old wits," for they seldom ran across anyone who could rival their pithiness, their terseness of expression, or their style of pleasantry.[44] The old wits lent a measure of dignity to an evening as men of experience and achievement, not as eccentrics flitting around the edge of intellectual life, and they received respect because they represented an age when an engaging wit was coveted as the mark of a civilized man. Contentious discussion was inappropriate here. Mason records how on one evening at Mrs. Montagu's Jenyns "absolutely refused" to take the lead in her *conversazione*, pleading age and the loss of his "volatile spirits." By 1785, we find him berated by Hannah More at Mrs. Vesey's after Thomas Sheridan, father of the playwright, had abused the English poets because they had not "*written to the heart.*" Although she tried to nudge him into some kind of defense, he would say nothing.[45]

The only recorded exception to this customary diffidence was Jenyns's celebrated interview with the novelist Fanny Burney, who as a girl was privileged to grow up among the literary luminaries of her day. In her effusive descriptions of the evening entertainments she attended with her father, she often exaggerates the importance of routine occurrences, and her account of her introduction to Jenyns is no exception. Nevertheless, the episode illustrates something of Jenyns's behavior. When Fanny Burney's second novel, *Cecilia*, made a name for itself in 1782, Jenyns wrote a series of notes to Mrs. Ord, appealing for an introduction to the author; and though Fanny herself shrank from such panegyrics, her enchanted father, who fed upon her literary fame, arranged a meeting for January 1783.

As Fanny and her father arrived at the appointed time, the young author was abashed to find a large group assembled to witness the encounter. Everyone rose when she entered and stood staring as Soame Jenyns, dressed in a court suit of apricot-colored silk lined with white satin, shuffled from one end of the room to the other and entered into an elegant and formal tribute. Distracted by this time, Fanny followed her hostess around to be introduced to the guests. This ritual finished, Mrs. Ord called upon Jenyns again, and now, to the great delight of her father and with "the chivalrous courtesy that he seemed to think the call demanded," he began a lengthy analysis of her novels. Fanny could barely contain her embarrassment, and when the other guests continued to fuss over her, she tolerated the experience in the hope that one of her friends would rescue her. No one dared interfere, however, for as Mrs. Thrale told her afterward, she had been "publicly destined" for Jenyns. Before the guests departed, Jenyns thought it necessary to recapitulate, leaving Fanny thoroughly overwhelmed by the time the evening finished.[46] Clearly, Mrs. Ord had mismanaged the event, and Jenyns had shown himself in a bad light. As George Cambridge explained apologetically to her the following day, she had seen him at a disadvantage. "His conversation is not flowing or regular," he said, "but nobody has more wit in occasional sallies."[47] If people had sat conversing in the customary way, things would have gone well, he suggested. But Fanny had trouble comprehending this remark, and "fagged" by the fuss the night before, she shook her head in dismay.

The event was an unfortunate one for Jenyns, who enjoyed the affection of the bluestockings and who, in his last years, basked in the glow of his reputation as a religious writer. He was by far the oldest and the most venerable of the habitués, and his earnest Christianity suited the ladies' unctuous piety. Even after he passed his eightieth birthday, he remained in good health and his mind continued alert. A year before his death, following the attempted assassination of George III, he brought his wife to London to congratulate the king on his escape and, awakening his muse from "a long slumber," presented the monarch with a copy of some lines he had composed as a celebration. Flushed with the warm reception he received, he reported to Hardwicke, "I made a Bow & had some Conference w^{t} his Majesty, & a much longer on the Terrass at Windsor on the next Sunday Evening, when his Majesty wth his usual Condescension, was extremely gracious to us both."[48] Having slept at the castle, he assessed it in his journal as "an exceeding good Inn." This visit proved to be his last public engagement. On a subsequent trip to London in December 1787, he developed a heavy fever from which he did not have the strength to recover and died on 18 December.[49]

Those who witnessed his advocacy of Christianity and who shared the years of his retirement voiced their despair. Gloom hung over the bluestocking circle. "The world has lost an ingenious author and his friends and society a most amiable man," wrote Mrs. Montagu. "I pity his widow greatly; they were always together and always good humoured and affectionate."[50] The pious Hannah More took great comfort in reflecting that he had died a sincere believer, unobscured by the doubts that had supposedly hung over him for so many years; and the bishop of London regretted the loss of one who could make the "fashionable world" read books of religion.[51] Finally, at the midnight burial in Bottisham church on 27 December, the vicar of Bottisham swerved from his customary succinctness to record in the parish register the loss of a man he admired as "one of the most blameless of Men, and one of the truest of *Christians*." On the south wall of Bottisham church, near the place in which he was buried, there is a monument designed by John Bacon, R.A., bearing this inscription:

> His amiable and benevolent temper,
> The superior powers of his understanding,

Accompany'd with an uncommon brilliancy of the truest and chastest wit,
His exemplary moral Character, his able defence of CHRISTIANITY, whose rules he uniformly practic'd
Were all such excellency's in him, as will survive, with an affectionate
And deep regret for his loss in the remembrance of those with whom he liv'd.
When they are no more, POSTERITY will know from his writings, The justness of the Sketch here drawn of his Character.

Let us now turn to those writings more fully.

Chapter Four
Poetry

Dodsley's *Collection*

The most famous collection of contemporary poetry published in England during the first half of the eighteenth century was Dodsley's *Collection of Poems. By Several Hands*, an anthology published in three volumes in 1748 and later expanded to three more. This venture was the triumph of the bookseller Robert Dodsley, a man of taste and a shrewd businessman with a knack for discovering new poetic talent likely to appeal to the reading public. The *Collection* therefore proved to be an interesting mixture of traditional poetry from the early part of the century, cleaving to neoclassical standards of correctness, and later poems attempting to escape the authority of those standards, notably in the more inventive and imaginative ode. It was an immediate success. Dodsley had not only solicited poems from those he judged to be the fashionable writers of the day but compiled a selection from earlier poets, such as Pope. Poets of reputation thus stood side by side with their lesser-known brethren; men barely able to make a living jostled with those of substance and rank. Among the contributors there was Mark Akenside and Lord Bolingbroke, Isaac Hawkins Browne and R. O. Cambridge, Lord Chesterfield and William Collins, John Dyer and Henry Fielding, Garrick and Gray, Johnson and Lyttelton, Mason and Pope, Thomas Tickell and Horace Walpole. And there was Soame Jenyns. To introduce Jenyns to his readers, Dodsley had seized upon a handful of the verses circulated in the manuscript dedicated to Lady Margaret Cavendish Harley and printed them together with the satiric pieces published separately in the intervening years. As a result, the venture did more than anything else to establish the name of Jenyns as a minor talent.

The sampling from "Poems on Several Occasions" possesses a gentlemanly, amateurish quality more typical of a man of leisure occupying his time than a serious poet seeking a reputation. Written from an upper-class point of view, these light exhibitions of verbal skill are chiefly love lyrics drawing on stock situations and peopled with conventional figures. And though they are love poems, they are charming rather than passionate in their treatment of love. In every instance, the mistress is politely treated as an object and love itself as an appetite that gives rise to playfulness. They are clearly aimed at the genteel reader. The satirical poems selected by Dodsley break away from the conventions of genteel love poetry and exhibit Jenyns's interest in burlesque and mock-heroic through such forms as the "art" poem and the "progress" poem. These later compositions are distinguished by their use of parody, irony, and wit, features that would prove to be characteristic of Jenyns's light-hearted treatment of social behavior from that point onward. For Jenyns was seldom grave. Rather, he interested himself in the manners of polite society and, in following that interest, failed to adopt the devices introduced by more serious and innovative poets, including the allegorical use of abstractions, the contemplation of landscape, the cult of the sublime, narrative poetry, or the so-called "romantic" tendencies of Gray and Collins. He never published a sonnet, though the form was revived, and he publicly ridiculed the Pindaric ode. With his conventional poetic diction, his conciseness of expression, and his admiration of the classics, he belongs to that group of poets of the early eighteenth century sometimes referred to as "Augustan." Working within the conventions of strict poetic forms, he has left a number of poems that are pleasing and entertaining even now.

With his love of burlesque and mimicry, Jenyns was particularly attracted to those two contemporary forms the classical imitation and the translation, forms that assumed the reader's knowledge of Latin. As a member of an educated minority, Jenyns had acquainted himself with the classical poets as well as their English imitators, and these had helped him establish a literary voice from the beginning. As long as a taste for classical imitation prevailed, Jenyns's poetry also continued to be read, and for a generation after Jenyns died, no major collection of British poets appeared without a generous selection of it. By that time, the taste in poetry had changed fundamentally; but while he lived, he wrote as "a man speaking to men like himself,"[1] as James Sutherland has put it: upper-class men who shared his tastes and interests, his reading, and his point of view. Jenyns handled with ease the experience he shared with people of education and position. Even satiric poems like "The Modern Fine Gentleman" and "The Modern Fine Lady" do not so much engender disapproval as gently mock two types of individual familiar to his own social group.

When we look at the other contributions to Dodsley's *Collection*, we may see why the editor could place Jenyns comfortably among them. They do not always represent the best poetry of the time, but they do let us know what was being read. Dodsley's poets were men of culture, and Dodsley assumed that his readers would savor their allusiveness and their stylized handling of nature and feeling. Just as their diction was the diction that had come to pervade English poetry from the last decade of the seventeenth century, Jenyns's earlier poetry features streams that are "silver," mountains that are a vivid "purple," nights that are "sable," and excited bosoms that "fire" according to the convention acknowledged by poets and readers alike. Later on, Jenyns chooses his words more freely—even colloquially. The sweetness of tone gives way to a gentle mockery inspired by Horace and Pope. The bulk of the collected poems, then, consists of the early amatory verse interspersed with occasional social satire, while here and there one finds complimentary *vers de société* and one or two philosophical discourses.

Early Verse

When Soame Jenyns arrived at Cambridge in 1722, the library of St. John's College had just taken possession of the books and papers of Matthew Prior, who had died the year before. At the time, Prior had no rival in the writing of occasional light verse, and his memory was undiminished. As Jenyns confessed, Prior was one of the models for his earliest poetry, a selection of which survives in "Poems on Several Occasions," light verse that approaches the subject of love in a familiar and facetious manner. Like Prior's, Jenyns's love poetry is epigrammatic and witty, often featuring a turn in the last stanza. Love is a game that engages the ingenuity of the lover without entangling the emotions. Like the verse of the Restoration court wits, the dandyish circle that made the writing of verse a modish, gentlemanly pursuit, Jenyns's treatment of love concerns itself with its physical intricacies. Thus, the object of desire is frequently portrayed as a cold, unyielding individual whose superficial modesty must be exposed and consequently overcome. The manuscript volume was full of such charming drawing room exercises calculated to please the cultivated circle at Wimpole Hall, the seat of Lady Margaret's father, the earl of Oxford, and the most splendid house in Cambridgeshire.

"Poems on Several Occasions" begins with two poems written in the spirit of panegyric. The first, a dedicatory epistle addressed to Lady Margaret Cavendish Harley, reviews the practice among the Ancients of dedicating poetry to fair women and compliments the lady as one deserving such attention even though she is the daughter of a literary patron. We glimpse the beginning of Jenyns's subtle irony here as he proceeds to compliment the earl of Oxford himself and finishes with the hope that these "children sprung from idleness and love" will be equally acceptable to him. He writes,

> Cou'd they, (but ah how vain is the design!)
> Hope to amuse your hours, as once they've mine,
> Th' ill-judging world's applause, and critics blame,
> Alike I'd scorn: your approbation's fame.
>
> (1:128)

The second poem, "Written in the Right Honourable the Earl of Oxford's Library at Wimple," is a tribute to the magnificent library constructed at Wimpole Hall, which was only about half a day's journey from Bottisham and a place that

Jenyns liked to visit. Here Oxford preserved one of the most impressive collections of books and manuscripts in the country in the library he completed in 1721, probably the most important private library ever assembled in Britain—so costly that Oxford's zeal as a collector depleted his resources. In 1741, when he was forced to sell Wimpole Hall, the nation acquired his precious collection of manuscripts, which remains intact as part of the holdings of the British Library. Oxford was not only a collector but a patron of scholars, artists, and writers, including Pope, Swift, and Prior, and Jenyns himself liked to associate himself with the literary milieu he created. This poem is a tribute to Oxford as one who has provided a home for learning at a time when it has been chased from court and Parliament. It compares him to the Roman literary patron Mecaenas:

> See OXFORD smiles! and all the tuneful train,
> In his Britannia's sons revive again;
> PRIOR, like HORACE, strikes the sounding strings,
> And in harmonious POPE once more great MARO sings.
> (1:33)

While these excessive claims must be read in the spirit of encomium, this poem is one of the few to celebrate what was a golden age at Wimpole Hall.

Two other poems from the remainder of the volume are worth mentioning here mainly because they are not typical of its general tone. "Written in His Grace the Duke of Buckingham's Works," a tribute to the second earl of Buckingham, a statesman whose works were published in 1704, stands out because it does not appear in the printed collection of Jenyns's poetry. Jenyns followed such poets as Dryden and Pope in drawing attention to this important statesman of the Revolution, though he does so uncritically, as we see in these lines:

> Without one slip Life's Icy path he trod,
> True to his prince, his Country, and his God;
> His faith was just, and his Religion such,
> As nere beleiv'd too little, or too much;
> Such as no Zeal, or prejudice cou'd blind,
> The sure resolves of a reflecting Mind.[2]

Buckingham was indeed an extraordinary man but not the paragon of virtue portrayed here, as his life of wasted talent and aimlessness shows. Curiously, though Jenyns revised the manuscript poems later in life, this one remained as it was. One other occasional poem left out of the collected works but worth noting is "On the Marchioness of Carmarthen's Recovery from the Small Pox," a single experiment with supernatural machinery. In this poem, the lady is praised as a beauty capable of rivaling Venus, and as the tissuey framework of the poem unfolds, Venus prays to Death to call forth the disease. The disease takes hold, and

> From her fair cheeks, to paint her own,
>   The fading rose the Goddess steals;
> Then smiling calls her little Son,
>   And from her eyes his quiver fills.[3]

As Death is about to pierce her heart, Fate stops the blow, arguing that the lady's charms have taken their share of victims as well and that she must be spared. With Death reproved, the distemper flies.

For the most part, the volume is a collection of amatory verses exhibiting an early preference for euphemism and circumlocution and worked out principally within the confines of the couplet. "To a Lady in Town, Soon After Her Leaving the Country" reverses the pattern of Pope's epistle to Miss Blount on her leaving town after the coronation. Whereas Pope's lonesome lover demeans the tamer joys of country life from his vantage point in the city street, Jenyns's seeks comfort in the joys of the country to relieve his "cruel pangs." But the music of Handel and Corelli fail to soothe him because music is "the voice of love"; the poetry of Pope and Prior makes matters worse with its pathetic scenes of woe; a walk by the Cam merely brings back pleasant memories; and the pleasures of the races at Newmarket fail to provide a distraction. Retreating to a book by the fire, he daydreams; and in the same way Pope is brought back to reality by a tap on the shoulder, he is jolted from his reverie when a weighty folio slips from his hands and crashes to the floor. This poem contains one or two sketches of the fields around Cambridge and a glimpse of the gaming tables at

Newmarket and exhibits an early attempt at imitation. "To a Lady, Sent with a Present of Shells and Stones Designed for a Grotto" is also a complimentary poem and one that goes a step further in celebrating country life. The shells are presented as "gaudy trifles," sportings of divine creation whose hidden glories will be doubly exposed when they are arranged according to the lady's taste. This leads the poet to a general consideration of the kind of woman who is able to take pleasure in natural objects in preference to the distractions of the city: who prefers the outdoors to the velvet chair, the nightingale to the opera singer, and the pages of a book to the excitement of the assembly room. It is an idealized portrait by a country poet who has not yet developed a taste for the world outside rural Cambridgeshire. "To a Lady, in Answer to a Letter Wrote in a Very Fine Hand" is another tribute worked out through a conceit: finding the "exactest image" of the maid in her exquisite letters. Our correspondent strives to copy her hand in vain, and he tells us resignedly at the end, "Believe me, fair, I'm practising this art, / To steal your hand, in hopes to steal your heart" (1:125). The last poem of this type, "To a Young Lady, Going to the West Indies," is an early attempt at mock-heroic marking the departure of a young charmer and comparing her progress to a journey of universal conquest. Soon, the poet jests, she, like Alexander the Great, will have conquered all mankind in the known world only to find that she has run out of things to conquer.

The remainder of "Poems on Several Occasions" offers other exercises in light verse, only a few of which need be mentioned here. "Written in a Lady's Volume of Tragedies" asks why "imaginary scenes of woe" cause distress so easily while the complaints of the helpless lover continue to be ignored, and "Written in Mr. Locke's Essay on Human Understanding" fixes the importance of Locke's discourse on the workings of the mind by ranking it with Eve's first view of herself in the water. However, "The Way to be Wise," an imitation of a fable by La Fontaine, is quite different. It is both an early instance of Jenyns's preference for the gentlemanly art of imitation and a foretaste of the ironic situation common in his maturer poetry. Here, a woman of the world retires to a convent to escape her tainted career and proceeds to live an exemplary life. When she is held up to the others as a model of piety, a young "slut" quickly points out that such wisdom could have come only from the kind of sordid experience the rest of them would be loath to try. And finally, "The Choice," which in language and design follows closely upon Pomfret's "Choice" (1700), is a catalog of female virtues meant to describe the perfect woman—one who is not only beautiful but charitable, skillful, and honorable. Above all, she is subservient and capable of rising above common female diversions like scandal-mongering so as to become "more than woman-kind."

If the poems examined so far are distinguished by their politeness and restraint, that does not mean Jenyns was incapable of treating the subject of love in an earthier manner. Other items from the collection are far more lascivious than these. "To a Nosegay in Pancharilla's Breast," a translation from Bonfonius reminiscent of Prior's "Love Disarmed," is a successful little erotic fantasy that considers what it would be like to change places with a senseless flower decorating a lady's bosom. Then it takes the reader on a journey of exploration:

> I'd never rest till I had found
> Which globe was softest, which most round—
> Which was most yielding, smooth, and white,
> Or the left bosom or the right;
> Which was the warmest, easiest bed,
> And which was tip'd with purest red.
> (1:37)

Not content with this, our explorer would descend lower still so as to rove "O'er all the fragrant Cyprian grove" but retreats in despair, realizing that these wishes can never be fulfilled. A translation from Anacreon, ode 20, continues in the same manner. This time the fantasy allows the admirer to change places with the lady's intimate garments so that he is left "Pleas'd, to be ought, that touches you, / Your glove, your garter, or your shoe" (1:165).

There are three other brief songs on the subject of seduction, the best of which begins, "Cease, Sally, thy charms to expand." It is distinguished from the others by its rollicking, hearty anapests, a rare variation of meter that combines with colloquial language to convey the earthy appeal of a tempting wench:

> Oh! Torture me not, for Love's sake,
>   With the smirk of those delicate lips,
> With that head's dear significant shake,
>   And the toss of the hoop and the hips.
>
> Oh! sight still more fatal! look there
>   O'er her tucker what murderers peep!
> So—now there's an end of my care,
>   I shall never more eat, drink, or sleep.
>   (1:145)

Of the remaining poems in this collection, one other demands our attention: "The Temple of Venus," a rapturous idealization of an island of love. This poem is unusual for its descriptive quality and its free use of the imagination. This is how the temple appears:

> Its walls a trickling fountain laves,
>   In which such virtue reigns,
> That, bath'd in its balsamic waves,
>   No lover feels its pains.
>
> Before th' unfolding gates there spreads
>   A fragrant spicy grove,
> That with its curling branches shades
>   The labyrinths of Love.
>   (1:171)

Jenyns did not attempt such smoothness and vividness again. His imagination was more suited to such ironic forms as the translation, imitation, burlesque, parody, and mock-heroic, and these dominated his mature verse.

Mature Verse

Most of the poems by Jenyns published in Dodsley's *Collection* were satirical and philosophical poems already in print, beginning with "The Art of Dancing" (1729). More mature and more competent, they demonstrated a shift of interest from light subjects to social and political behavior. While Jenyns continued to indulge his facility for wit, he now developed further his technique of frequent reference to well-known classical and contemporary poets by way of paraphrase and burlesque. By means of this technique, he established a pattern of verbal allusion and suggestion, harking back to works that would be recognized by the educated reader. It was to become an essential part of his satiric wit and energy. This kind of poetry also retained the authority of tradition, for it suggested a sympathy for the moral and rational attitude of the classics, with their lessons of everyday prudence.

"The Art of Dancing" (1729), Jenyns's longest and most ambitious poem and the first to be published, illustrates both an affinity for mild satire and a complex use of allusion in support of it. The vogue for the "art" poem may be traced to Horace's "Art of Poetry" and Ovid's "Art of Love." From classical models such as these, satirical burlesque imitations flourished throughout the eighteenth century, maintaining the same didactic purpose but offering something else: technical precepts of the particular "art" under discussion, extended similes, invocations, and moral parallels. Jenyns may well have been familiar with such precursors as Dr. William King's "Art of Cookery" [1708] and James Bramston's "Art of Politicks" (1729), for in keeping with their didactic pretension he too asserts that his own poem consists of "useful lines" of his "instructive" muse. Instances of parody appear early. The reader is reminded of Pope's *Essay on Criticism* (1711) in couplets like "True dancing, like true wit, is best exprest / By nature only to advantage drest" and "The dance and music must so nicely meet, / Each note should seem an echo to your feet" (1:20–21). Gay's *Trivia* (1716) is the likely source of the mock-mythological episode concerning the origin of the fan (Gay's Patty, for whom Vulcan made the patten, suggesting Jenyns's Fanny, for whom Aeolus made the fan). Gay's clever lines at the end of *Trivia* are closely parodied, beginning with the identical line "And now compleat my gen'rous Labours lie" in the original version.

Canto I begins with formal classical features: a proposition and an invocation addressed to Venus and Jove. Then there is a short essay on the rise and progress of dancing, followed by an encomium upon the Ancients (who admired dancing as an art) and suddenly some useful dressing hints for the young spark. Clean white gloves and smelling salts "to raise the fainting fair" are recommended as essential equipment, but powdered wigs are ruled out since they are likely to ruin the lady's lace, and unprotected shoe buckles are viewed as a threat to stockings and petticoats. Above all, the gentleman is cautioned,

> Let not the Sword, in silken Bondage ty'd,
> An useless Weight, hang lugging at your Side;
> No such rough Weapons here will gain the Prize,
> No Wounds we fear, but from the Fair-one's Eyes.[4]

As for the ladies, they receive a warning against painting the face, and in lines that parody Pope's *Dunciad Variorum* (1728) they learn that the effect produced on their faces will be similar to that of melting snow on a fine spring day:

> Then strait at once the glitt'ring Scenes decay,
> And all the transcient Glories fade away;
> The Fields resign the Beauties not their own,
> And all their Snowy Charms run trickling down.[5]

Lappets, ruffles, fringes, and other paraphernalia are forbidden—particularly the fashionable hoop, a popular article of clothing but the instrument of numerous casualties. "Oft hath my self the Inconvenience found; / Oft have I trod th' immeasurable Round, / And mourn'd my Shins bruis'd black, with many a Wound," the poet reveals.[6] A warning to the ladies about the need to tie fast their garters introduces a short historical diversion on the Order of the Star and Garter, instituted by Edward III, and Canto I ends with a descriptive encomium on the fan with an episode detailing its invention by Aeolus.

As the rest of the poem progresses (Canto II and Canto III in the first edition), the glittering dancers arrange themselves about the assembly room and settle down to enjoy the evening. A ball must begin with formal French dancing—the Rigadoon and the Louvre, the Borée and the Courant, the Minuet and the Bretagne—and so the French are praised for inventing these fashionable ballroom movements, especially Fuillet, who devised the first dance notation. A lecture follows, advising each dancer to measure his own capabilities to decide, like the poet who sets out to write, whether to attempt what is more intricate or to maintain the "easie pace" of simpler forms. Next comes a short interlude on stage dancing and rope dancing, then basic rules of deportment scorning effeminacy in men and coquettishness in women, and everyone is cautioned about the need to maintain strict time.

With the formal part of the evening out of the way, we now turn to country dancing and, in keeping with the presumed didactic intention of the work, begin with the rise and progress of this pursuit, which is compared to the early development of the theater. There are hints for choosing a partner, and these lead inevitably by way of a neat analogy to the choice of a wife. Beauty is certainly desirable, Jenyns observes, but it is better in the long run to marry for "merit" so as to avoid some of the common burdens of married life:

> Unhappy is that hopeless Wretch's Fate
> Who, fetter'd in the Matrimonial State,
> With a poor, simple, unexperienc'd Wife
> Is forc'd to lead the tedious Dance of Life:
> And such is his with such a Partner join'd;
> A moving Puppet, but without a Mind:
> Still must his Hand be pointing out the Way,
> Yet ne'er can teach so fast as she can stray;
> Beneath her Follies he must ever groan,
> And ever blush for Errors not his own.[7]

There is sensible advice here. Even more is to be learned about the nature of women from "Hunt-the-Squirrel," a country dance in which the lady "Seeks when we fly, but flies when we pursue," and the round dance, one that presumably reveals the inconstancy of women by its rapid changing of partners. At this point, the philosopher is invited to glimpse the workings of the universe in the near approach and separation of the dancers and the moralist to discern the vanity of human labor as the sweating crowd ends up in the same order in which it began. There are a few comments on the presence of the elders, whose attendance is apt to dampen the spirits of the young, and finally some careful advice about keeping out the chill on the way home, with a special warning about the effects of beer drinking. A formal conclusion thus brings to an end a highly successful and entertaining specimen of the "art" poem, blending moral insight and realistic detail and providing an interesting study of an important social pastime.

Dodsley next selected from his inventory "An Epistle, Written in the Country, to the Right Hon. the Lord Lovelace then in Town" (1735), a descriptive-philosophical nature poem of a kind that had become common in the early eighteenth century, one that combined a "Horatian" mood of retirement with a feeling of contentment with everyday pleasures. Jenyns, with his rollicking Hudibrastic couplets, takes the form a step further as he introduces his characteristic irony and turns the poem into a description of the more raucous country pastimes for the benefit of a friend in the city. In the last half of the poem, he directs some of the fun at himself with a self-portrait of an uncharacteristically bookish squire who shrinks from the society of his neighbors.

The poem opens with a nostalgic look back to a golden age when country life was more settled, when nymphs were chaste and swains were true, and it bewails the fact that the country has since become a center of discord. It is no longer a place of virtue and innocence, Jenyns contends. Girls are no longer chaste, justices and squires differ over jurisdiction, attorneys exact inflated profits, and neighbors quarrel over rates, tithes, and game. Not even the dignity of the church has remained intact. The strife of living in the country is unbearable, the squire maintains, and so are its diversions,

> For seldom I with 'squires unite,
> Who hunt all day and drink all night;
> Nor reckon wonderful inviting,
> A quarter-sessions, or cock-fighting.
> (1:42)

The preoccupation of militiamen, sheriffs, and other worthies with honors and ceremonies comes in for a good deal of ridicule, and so do the dinners of overbred knights, which fall flat with dullness and snobbery.

Jenyns's description of the flurry of activity set off when a neighbor casually drops in unannounced, hoping to avoid the customary ceremonial of the shires, is good farce. At that moment the whole household erupts, and the event becomes a vignette of rural behavior, beginning with a parody of the half-comic distress introducing Pope's "Epistle to Dr. Arbuthnot," published the same year. No reader could fail to recognize the source of this passage, uttered by the lady of the house as she panics at the sight of her visitors:

> JOHN, JOHN, a coach!—I can't think who 'tis,
> My lady cries, who spies your coach,
> Ere you the avenue approach;
> Lord, how unlucky!—washing day!
> And all the men are in the hay!
> (1:43)

There follow a fit of confusion, the sound of scurrying feet, and "three hours of tedious waiting" before dinner arrives, the foretaste of a dull evening featuring the tipsy knight lecturing his guests on the evils of governments.

All this prepares the reader for the second half of the poem, neatly balancing the first half with a parody of the last fifty lines of Prior's "Epistle to Fleetwood Shepherd," the description of the leisurely life of a young tutor that Jenyns turns into an account of how he spends his time "The circulating hours dividing / 'Twixt reading, walking, eating, riding." It is a picture of retirement and ease, of a life occupied with reading not only travel books, history, and religious controversy but the scientific works of Newton and Boyle. These eclectic reading tastes do not complete the picture, however, for our man of leisure is also content to pass his time indolently in meditation or in wandering through the countryside, spinning out the hours in temperance and moderation. And so, with a hint of self-ridicule, he gently prods his companion to abandon the wearying follies of the city and visit a "dull country friend," finishing with the offer of these rural diversions:

> A house, where quiet guards the door,
> No rural wits smoke, drink, and roar,
> Choice books, safe horses, wholesome liquor,
> Clean girls, backgammon, and the vicar.
>   (1:49)

For the next decade, Jenyns did not write a single poem with the same ironic edge. After spending a session in Parliament observing the London social and political scene from close range, he next turned out a pair of poems that displayed not only breadth and maturity but a shift of interest from parochial Cambridgeshire to London. Jenyns had a particularly good eye for social pretension, and he revealed his insights first in "The Modern Fine Gentleman" (1746) and then in its companion piece "The Modern Fine Lady" (1750), the first included in Dodsley's *Collection* and the second added by Dodsley to the fourth volume in 1755. Both were polished specimens of the "progress" poem, a biographical set piece well established as a vehicle for satire at this time. "The Modern Fine Gentleman," a series of "characters" drawn from Jenyns's acquaintance with the fop, the naive politician, and the clever sharper, follows in the path of Tom Rakewell in Hogarth's "Rake's Progress" and Sir Fopling Flutter, the man of fashion featured in Etherege's *Man of Mode* (1676). Gay had attempted something similar in "The Birth of the Squire." Jenyns's immediate model was probably the portrait of Sir Balaam in Pope's "Epistle to Bathurst" (1733), a poem it resembles in both phraseology and design.[8]

The poem is the best example of Jenyns's skill at manipulating well-known character types and parodying lines of well-known verse for satiric purposes. We first encounter the young hero as he finishes school and completes the Grand Tour, returning home full of conventional knowledge but qualified to do nothing useful. In lines that echo the contradictions of Dryden's Zimri, he is

> A monster of such complicated worth,
> As no one single clime could e'er bring forth;

> Half atheist, papist, gamester, bubble, rook,
> Half fidler, coachman, dancer, groom, and cook.
> (1:65)

A parliamentary career seems to be the only appropriate pursuit for a man of such varied accomplishments, and soon he purchases a seat for himself on the strength of his status as a country gentleman, installing himself in the Commons ostentatiously attired in his modish French garb and delivering himself of wild libertarian speeches attacking government. Yet he supports no particular cause. With another clever parody of the Thames quatrain from Denham's "Cooper's Hill," perhaps the most parodied lines in eighteenth-century verse, Jenyns explains,

> Forth from his lips, prepar'd at all to rail,
> Torrents of nonsense burst, like bottled ale,
> Tho' shallow, muddy; brisk, tho' mighty dull;
> Fierce without strength; o'erflowing, tho' not full.
> (1:66)

Pleased with his own sense of worth, the young parliamentarian would have himself thought a sophisticated gambler, but after each excursion to White's Club he usually ends up disowning his debts. He stoops to cheating, and when he mortgages his estate and sells his timber to raise cash, he discovers he has nothing left with which to purchase votes and consequently loses his seat. In desperation, he marries an aged widow, only to find that she has been willed a fixed income instead of an estate,[9] and finally allows himself to be bought off by the ministry he had previously deplored. Stripped of his independence, he suffers the disdain of both Whigs and Tories; but assured of a steady income again, he lends out money at outrageous rates and lives out his days in the less dignified station of a parasite. The parasite is the last of the series of "characters" contrived by Jenyns to create what is perhaps his most artistically satisfying poem. The slow decline of the would-be politician presents a dismal prospect indeed, and the epigrammatic quality of the couplets has no equal elsewhere in his poetry.

The superiority of "The Modern Fine Gentleman" is more obvious when it is compared to "The Modern Fine Lady," a moral tale about the consequences of pride. Instead of a series of vignettes, Jenyns presents this time the character of a high-born lady of libertine temperament whose sense of superiority leads her into a life of gambling and amorous intrigues and ultimately to a lonely and ignominious death. Bred to quality, she sees her youth slip by through one diversion after another while she acquires the social arts and the skills of coquetry: "For this she listens to each fop that's near, / Th' embroider'd colonel flatters with a sneer, / And the cropt ensign nuzzles in her ear" (1:73). Exhausted by these amusements, she mistakenly condescends to marry an ambitious country squire in desperation, adding spiritual degeneracy to financial decline. But when she feels no satisfaction with the measured pace of family life and "no transports in the bridal-bed," she prostitutes herself out of curiosity and eventually returns to the frantic round of cards, until once again she loses her possessions. The poignant climax of the poem arrives as we observe her borne unashamedly back to her husband's country estate, where the tenants and servants celebrate her return with bonfires and bell-ringing. She, on the other hand, disdains to notice them:

> Silent and sullen, like some captive queen,
> She's drawn along unwilling to be seen,
> Until at length appears the ruin'd *Hall*
> Within the grass-green moat and ivy'd wall,
> The doleful prison where for ever she,
> But not, alas! her griefs, must bury'd be.
> (1:76)

Bereft of her diversions, she sinks into a peevish decline, shunned by those around her and robbed of her last prerogative, insulting the curate's callous wife. There is less amusement and less satiric sharpness in this poem, and the gravity of tone is unusual. But taken together, the two progress poems achieve a satisfactory balance and demonstrate what Jenyns might have achieved as a serious poet before he turned his hand to exclusively political verse and to prose.

Dodsley's *Collection* also made public for the first time a poem called "An Essay on Virtue," a purely philosophical poem embracing a set of ethical principles that found their fullest expression in *A Free Inquiry into the Nature and Origin of Evil* (1757). "An Essay on Virtue" was part of the vogue enjoyed by the doctrine of "benevolence" set forth by the third earl of Shaftesbury in *Characteristicks of Men, Manners, Opinions, Times* (1711), a doctrine that represents a turning point in the history of ethics. While it remained fashionable, it created a quickening of interest in the problems of mankind among major and minor writers alike.[10] James Thomson was one of its advocates, and through Thomson, Shaftesbury reached many other poets, notably Shenstone, Savage, and Akenside. While these poets do not always cite their source, the similarity of their preoccupations is nevertheless apparent. At the beginning of the eighteenth century, when many of those who had lost their faith to the claims of the New Science resorted to skepticism, the change did not discourage theological speculation. Disputes over such issues as the existence of evil and the nature of conscience continued, and one way of explaining the discrepancies between natural philosophy and religion (see chapter 6) was to find a moral pattern in Nature's design and to fashion oneself after it by adopting some discipline or way of life. One possible guide to behavior emerged from Shaftesbury's writings, for Shaftesbury offered an alternative to both self-interest and the church's system of rewards and punishments. Man, he claimed, possessed a "natural" moral sense. Everything in the universe was ordered or regulated for the best by a managing deity whose designing principle was necessarily good and permanent.

"An Essay on Virtue" is notable for its adherence to Shaftesburian doctrine and its outright dissatisfaction with Christian ethics. At the beginning of the poem, Jenyns dismisses popular notions of virtue by asserting what it is not—a quality possessed by one who claims to possess it:

> Hence youth good-humour, frugal craft old-age,
> Warm politicians term it party-rage,
> True churchmen zeal right orthodox; and hence
> Fools think it gravity, and wits pretence;

> To constancy alone fond lovers join it,
> And maids unask'd to chastity confine it.
>
> (1:54)

While each of us may define virtue through his own behavior, Jenyns claims, virtue is really a rule of life, a desire to spread God's goodness throughout Creation. Here for the first time, he supports his argument with the concept of the Great Chain of Being, the theory of creation that teaches "In ev'ry tract of ocean, earth, and skies, / Myriads of creatures still successive rise" and take their appointed places within God's grand design. Consequently, each creature in its own station promotes the general good—each one except Man, the one species that delights in inflicting pain. Having learned the principle of "common welfare" in the first half of the poem, we encounter an objection from a Puritan divine "Whose well-stuffed cheeks with ease and plenty shine." To be virtuous, he argues, is to fast and to mortify the flesh, to work out one's salvation through fear and pain. God is cruel and severe, and he has placed man in the world simply to sojourn before he is committed to hell. In contrast to this view, Jenyns presents an image of God as "universal parent" and the world as a "sportive nursery," an "instant state" that man is meant to enjoy while he takes the opportunity to earn "superior bliss" in some afterlife. Most of our ills we bring upon ourselves, says Jenyns, and in the last section of the poem he describes an ideal world in which the practice of virtue would eliminate error. The pious would not feel compelled to give up food or rest or to wear hair shirts to demonstrate their resolve, and no one would be asked to believe what reason contradicts. Instead, men would seek one another's good and therefore become what God had first intended them to be.

Jenyns reinforced these ideas in his elegant translation of Isaac Hawkins Browne's "De Animi Immortalitate," added to the fourth volume of Dodsley's *Collection* in 1758. While this is Browne's poem, the ideas are similar to those to be encountered in Jenyns's later philosophical writings, some of which appear here for the first time. Life itself is described variously as a "fair" where we cannot stay, an "inn" where we must wait, and a "sea" that is to take us to a port. It cannot be the reward of virtue, Browne continues, because evils exist despite our experience here. God is "supremely wise and just," and no matter how imperfect things may appear to us, the fact remains that whatever is, as Pope had put it, is right. Accordingly, the inference to be drawn is that there must exist some future state or else it would appear that evil triumphs. For just as there is a law of gravity affecting the bodies in the solar system, there is another one connecting the present and future states. Drawing on this scientific analogy further, the poem suggests that there is also a social law implying that when we all act virtuously together, we combine to do good like the force of gravity. Unlike the "Essay on Virtue," Jenyns appears to accept here, by acknowledging the existence of a future state, a system of rewards and punishments, a more orthodox view of divine justice.

Imitations

After his reelection in 1747, Soame Jenyns wrote fewer poems for publication and instead shifted to prose as a medium for discussing the philosophical and political issues that had begun to occupy his thoughts. He now confined himself to occasional light verse—a tribute to Lord Chesterfield, a celebration of Miss Yorke's marriage to Lord Anson, a panegyric addressed to the king after he had survived an attempt on his life—and political satire, particularly four "imitations" of Horace written during his second session in the Commons, three of them dedicated to the Yorkes. Burlesque imitations of classical poets formed part of the classical revival in progress in England during the early part of the eighteenth century, and these exercises in translation particularly appealed to poets like Jenyns, men who possessed the wit and skill to write but not the inclination to abandon completely their gentlemanly pursuits. Though these imitations are satiric, they lack a spirit of contentiousness and concentrate instead on the interpretation of life and conduct.

The challenge of this kind of poetry lay in bringing the original up to date without transforming its ideas, demonstrating that nature always remained the same even if the choice of words did not. The reader's pleasure depended on keeping in mind the words of the original while the poet paralleled the acknowledged model, subordinating it to his new poetic intention and taking, as Dryden had said, "only some general hints from the original, to run division on the groundwork, as he pleases."[11] Thus, the original was usually printed side by side with the imitation to allow the modern reader the full benefit of the translator's ingenuity. According to Jenyns, the chief feature of the burlesque imitation was "a lucky and humorous application of the words and sentiments of any author to a new subject totally different from the original" (1:81).

The kind of satire featured in such imitations is epistolary satire, the informal and familiar mode of social criticism associated with Horace and Pope and suited to Jenyns's own personality and talents. It does not lash or stab but endeavors to correct follies and errors through argument, insinuation, pleasantry, and good sense. It is, in short, gentlemanly satire. As Ambrose Philips phrased it in *Spectator* no. 618, the author must be "a Master of refined Raillery, and understand the Delicacies, as well as the Absurdities of Conversation. He must have a lively Turn of Wit, with an easie and concise manner of Expression; Every thing he says, must be in a free and disengaged manner."[12] This neatly summarizes Jenyns's satiric disposition. Richard Cumberland had Jenyns in mind when he wrote, "Raillery is of all weapons the most dangerous and two-edged; of course it ought never to be handled, but by a gentleman, and never should be played with, but upon a gentleman; the familiarity of a low-born vulgar man is dreadful; his raillery, his jocularity, like the shaking of a water-spaniel, can never fail to soil you with some sprinkling of the dunghill, out of which he sprung."[13] The four poems considered here are therefore genteel imitations of Horatian odes and epistles, familiar verse giving the impression of spontaneity in response to a pleasant or unpleasant event that might have taken place in the poet's life. They are strongly autobiographical in subject matter and colloquial in language, alerting the reader to human foibles and frailties, discoursing upon philosophical principles, revealing personal details, or describing everyday scenes and incidents.

The only imitation to be published separately was "An Ode to the Hon. Philip Y--ke, Esq." (1747), an imitation of Horace, book 2, ode 16, written after the election campaign of 1747. Ode 16 asserts that contentment with one's lot is the only true happiness. Horace opens with the reflection that just as the mariner cannot buy peace in a storm and the soldier peace in battle, treasure cannot buy peace for the soul. The happy man lives frugally and avoids disturbing his sleep with greed. He has learned that it is better to be happy in the present than to worry continually about what the future has in store. In conclusion, he presents a picture of his own state of mind, the mind of a man possessed of a modest estate, a love of poetry, and a scorn for envy. Placed side by side with this, the imitation proves to be concerned not with the philosophical contemplation of care but with the care that haunts politicians determined to stay in office. Since elections are a necessary evil to the politician, says Jenyns, elected members cannot seek immunity behind the speaker and the sergeant-at-arms when a new election is called but must worry about being thrown out of office. With the colloquial language consistent with his lighthearted tone, he asks,

> Why should we then to London run,
> And quit our chearful country sun
>   For business, dirt, and smoke?
> Can we, by changing place and air,
> Ourselves get rid of, or our care?
>   In troth 'tis all a joke.
>   (1:133)

Once a candidate is chosen, he should be able to relax. But each good brings with it a compensating ill, the poem teaches us, and "Elections are the devil." There follow the examples of Sir Robert Walpole and the earl of Bath, great men who lost their seats at the height of their powers, and the poem concludes with contrasting sketches of Jenyns's parliamentary colleague, Philip Yorke, and of Jenyns himself, the first a glimpse of aristocratic privilege and the second a self-deprecating picture of a country member worried by voters but favored by the gods. This added a highly personal note to a poem that caught the terror of the member faced with the task of reelection while it attempted to strike out in a direction different from its Latin original.

The second imitation addressed to Yorke, an imitation of book 4, ode 8, is not so successful. This time, Horace's ode takes up a well-established poetic theme, the power of poetry to outlast material honors. Again, the tone is personal. Horace begins by stating that he would gladly bestow expensive gifts on his friends if he could, but since his poetry is all he possesses, he must define its value. With a grand sweep, he shows that public monuments cut in marble would have been insufficient to record the deeds of heroes, the retreat of Hannibal, or the burning of Carthage without the assistance of the muse. Without the muse, the reputation of every hero worthy of renown would perish. Jenyns's imitation begins with the same offer to bestow the gifts that would match the poet's feeling of generosity and ends regretting he has only his verse to offer Yorke so that Yorke's deeds of public benevolence will not be lost. This more trivial composition was undoubtedly meant to amuse Yorke even though it took as its theme the power of rhyme to outstrip brass and stone, and it ended with one of Jenyns's characteristic comic turns:

> The muse forbids the brave to die,
> Bestowing immortality:
> Still by her aid in blest abodes
> ALCIDES feasts among the Gods;
> And royal ARTHUR still is able
> To fill his hospitable table
> With English beef, and English knights,
> And looks with pity down on WHITE'S.
> (1:141)

Far more amusing and satirically effective is the imitation of book 3, ode 9, "A Dialogue Between the Right Hon. Henry Pelham and Madam Popularity," a comic piece of wider application written in 1752 when the Pelham administration introduced the popular measure of reducing the land tax from three shillings to two. The land tax had been raised from two shillings to four in 1739, at the beginning of the war with Spain, and it continued at that rate until the Treaty of Aix-la-Chapelle in 1748. The following year, it dropped to three shillings, and it did not return to its original level for another three years. In the midst of the popular acclaim surrounding Henry Pelham at the time, Jenyns tossed off this imitation of the Horatian dialogue between Horace and "Lydia" that traced the reconciliation of two estranged lovers, one complaining that he has lost her affections and the other that she has had to take second place to "Chloe." Yes, Chloe does hold his heart, he confesses, and he would freely give his life for her. But when Lydia intimates that she in turn has lost her heart to Calais, there is a quickening of interest. What if fair Chloe were rejected and the door were opened again? Then, says Lydia, she would gladly live and die with him, though he is lighter than a cork and stormier than the Adriatic. These epithets were important to the satiric effect of the imitation. It paralleled the original closely, and its success depended on the reader's awareness of the estranged Madam Popularity's hostile tone of voice. Things were peaceful, says Pelham, when you were "constant, chaste and wise," but now you grant your favors to every knave or fool. She is offended, she replies, by having to take second place to Britannia and feels slighted because Pelham has devoted himself to delivering Britannia from the national debt, reducing the lending rate to three percent, keeping a standing army and, above all, maintaining the land tax at three shillings. As a result of this exchange, there is a compromise, and the poem concludes by capturing the flavor of the original:

> H. PELHAM
> Suppose now, Madam, I was willing
> For once to bate this grievous shilling,
> To humour you—I know 'tis wrong,
> But you have such a cursed tongue.
>
> MADAM POPULARITY
> Why then, tho' rough as winds or seas,
> You scorn all little arts to please,
> Yet thou art honest, faith, and I
> With thee alone will live and die.
> (1:197)

The most successful imitation was a rendering of one of Horace's best-known epistles, book 2, epistle 1, as Jenyns juxtaposed Horace's critical opinions of Roman poetry with his own observations of English politics, parodying now and then Pope's imitation of the same poem.[14] In spirit, it is quite different from those of Horace and Pope, both of which are serious apologies for poets in contrast to the prevailing tastes of Augustus and George II respectively. Jenyns's imitation praises Jenyns's patron, Lord Chancellor Hardwicke, as "the bright example of the age" and depends upon the conscious echo of its models for its humor. In fact, Jenyns goes so far as to warn the reader in his advertisement, "if he thinks it not worth while to compare it line for line with the original, he will find in it neither wit, humour, nor even common sense; all the little merit it can pretend to consisting solely in the closeness of so long, and uninterrupted an imitation" (1:81).

The reader should have considered not only the original, but the 1737 imitation of Pope, who had turned his into a satiric judgment of George II and the tastes of his age. In his review of the literature of both the preceding age and the present one, he had made a plea for an understanding of the role of the poet in society, concluding with an ironic yet good-natured panegyric addressed to the king, apologizing for its lack of zeal:

> But Verse alas! your Majesty disdains;
> And I'm not used to Panegyric strains:
> The Zeal of Fools offends at any time,
> But most of all, the Zeal of Fools in ryme.
> Besides, a fate attends on all I write,
> That when I aim at praise, they say I bite.[15]

Should he ever be reduced to such a position, Pope writes, he hopes his pages find a use in wrapping spices or lining trunks.

Previously, Horace had set out to demonstrate that Augustus was not the patron of poets in general but of those content to flatter him, and he had written his *apologia* to encourage Augustus to extend his patronage to the rest. In taking up the cause of his contemporaries against the taste of the time, the preferences of the court and nobility, and the values of the emperor himself, Horace had shown, by tracing the rise and progress of taste in Rome, how the practice of the polite arts in Greece had provided writers with advantages over their predecessors: how morals had been improved and licence restrained, how satire and comedy had proved to be socially useful, how the extravagances of the stage had accumulated because of poor taste, and how poets had proved they deserved a place. They alone would transmit the emperor's name to posterity.

Jenyns's imitation of Horace is quite different from Pope's. Instead of passing judgment on his patron, Hardwicke, Jenyns makes him the subject of panegyric at the outset, as he writes,

> With such unrivall'd eminence you shine,
> That in this truth alone all parties join,
> The seat of justice in no former reign
> Was e'er so greatly fill'd, nor ever can again.
> (1:85)

What follows is a good-natured look at political life following the election of 1747 and an assessment of contemporary practices that combines insights into the behavior of voters and politicians alike. Taking as an example the fate of Sir Robert Walpole, Jenyns observes how politicians are doomed never to gain respect during their lifetimes: "Great men whilst living must expect disgraces, / Dead they're ador'd—when none desire their places" (1:85). Historically, he recalls, the English squires dispensed justice and looked after their neighbors happily, but now they seek popularity by nursing voters. Taking his own career as an example of this, he confesses,

> Ev'n I, who swear these follies I despise,
> Than statesmen, or their porters, tell more lies;
> And, for the fashion-sake, in spite of nature,
> Commence sometimes a most important creature,
> Busy as CAR—W rave for ink and quills,
> And stuff my head and pockets full of bills.
> (1:95)

This modern taste in politics, he thinks, produces a new breed of politician who will take advantage of any opportunity to speak or fill up the magazines with essays or orations, turning Parliament itself into a form of entertainment for those too poor to attend a play or too bored to go to church.

In keeping with the pattern of its model, the poem continues with a review of election practices, moving from the harvest entertainments of the ancient gentry to the election entertainments of candidates and finally to the practice of buying votes. Touching on the current tendency for parliamentary reform, Jenyns notes that politicians must go out of their way to impress voters:

> Some think an int'rest may be form'd with ease,
> Because the vulgar we must chiefly please;
> But for that reason 'tis the harder task,
> For such will neither pardon grant, nor ask.
> (1:103)

These conservative ideas on the subject of reform do not receive full expression until his later prose works (see chapter 5), but even so Jenyns's position on reform at this point is succinctly put when he suggests that a politician who takes satisfaction from the applause of the mob will soon find himself changing with "ev'ry drunken cobler's" smile or frown. There are amusing sketches of a newly elected knight from a distant shire who takes pleasure in the spectacle and ritual of Parliament and of an "eloquent" statesman who plays to the benches, the one ignorant of what is really going on and the other unaware that he is boring his listeners. Though Jenyns confesses that he himself has "no gift of tongue," he asks,

> Is there a MAN whose eloquence has pow'r
> To clear the fullest house in half an hour,
> Who now appears to rave and now to weep,
> Who sometimes makes us swear, and sometimes sleep,
> Now fills our heads with false alarms from FRANCE,
> Then conjurer like to INDIA bids us dance?
> (1:107)

After all of this amusing realism, the poem concludes with a shift in tone as Jenyns offers a sincere encomium to

Hardwicke as patron of poets and an affected expression of his own insufficiency for the task. Parodying Pope, he recommends that these lines might find a use in wrapping up sugar loaves for Wimpole. Lines like these prompted Horace Walpole to label him "the Poet-laureate of the Yorkes."

Chapter Five
Political Writings
Soame Jenyns and the Whigs

Modern notions of party ideology and party discipline obscure for us now the concept of "party" in the eighteenth century, a time when the terms "Whig" and "Tory" were not clearly defined and when the application of such terms did not necessarily indicate how an individual member of Parliament was likely to vote. Certainly, the Whigs maintained themselves in power with their web of patronage long after they were installed by George II, leaving the Tories in opposition tainted with Jacobitism; but the Whigs were not a cohesive group, and because there were so many varieties of Whig, success in parliamentary politics called for the careful management of diverse factions. The principal faction traced its line of descent directly from the Revolution of 1688 to Walpole, Pelham, and Hardwicke and looked successively for leadership to Henry Pelham and the duke of Newcastle, though as time went on it ceased to define itself in terms of its revolutionary origins. Other factions, unwilling to appear pure party men, united behind the fourth duke of Bedford, George Granville, and William Pitt; others still, such as Lord North, drew their influence from the king.

Soame Jenyns survived as a government member for thirty-eight years within this system despite the shifts of power that characterized the great era of Whig supremacy. In the beginning, the Reverend William Cole tells us, he had sympathized with the Tories, as his father had, but when asked to stand for Parliament in 1742, he "diverted" to the Whigs[1] and, with his distaste for opposition, avidly supported each Whig leader in succession. Until 1755, he remained bound by his allegiance to his patron, Lord Hardwicke. When he accepted an appointment to the Board of Trade, he also became a government placeman, one of the grand array of nearly two hundred members of Parliament who gave their support to successive administrations in exchange for a substantial salary. These placemen provided each administration with debating strength while they exercised their abilities in a variety of minor posts. And though they could not form a government themselves without a national leader, they could certainly be relied upon to keep a leader in power. Once in office, the placeman was required to stand for reelection, but since his constituency was probably controlled by a local Whig manager, there was usually no obstacle to his reelection except expense. In this way, an administration in power protected the reelection of its supporters, as the career of Soame Jenyns illustrates.

Hardwicke deftly shifted Jenyns from a county seat to the rotten borough of Dunwich and then back to the town of Cambridge. Jenyns's account at Martin's Bank, London, which had maintained a modest balance of around £100, suddenly shot up to around £500 in 1755, when he began to receive his salary of £600, and it never fell below that level. His pass book shows that after retirement, he deposited in it close to £800 a year until his death.[2] The division lists preserved among the Newcastle papers fix him first as a country gentleman under the patronage of either Henry Pelham or Hardwicke, voting consistently with the administration, and then, with the fall of Newcastle, as a supporter of Fox against Pitt.[3] He also attached himself to the brief Rockingham administration in 1765–66.[4] As a result of these shifts, he has subsequently been dismissed as a party hack who turned out pamphlets at the direction of his patrons while suppressing his own views, but this was not the case. Jenyns did not rely upon his pen to keep himself in office. He remained a creature of the parliamentary system of the time and consistently subscribed to a set of conservative ideas about the nature of government. Before examining these ideas, it will be helpful to look at the doctrine that shaped Whig attitudes and influenced the passage of legislation. This doctrine originated with the political philosophy of John

Locke in his *Second Treatise of Government* (1690). Though written before 1688, this work subsequently gained authority as an interpretation of the Revolution settlement, effectively disposing of the Tory thesis of Divine Right; and although it did not influence the immediate supporters of the Revolution, it had achieved almost universal acceptance by the middle of the eighteenth century.[5]

While Locke had set out to refute polemically the absolutism of Sir Robert Filmer, Locke's carefully reasoned line of argument must be viewed as a political philosophy that shared a clear set of assumptions with those of other political philosophers. His opening remarks on a "state of nature," for example, echo those of a long series of writers stretching from the Ancients to more recent theorists such as Hobbes, Grotius, and Pufendorf, writers with whom he shared the common assumption of natural law. Within this philosophical tradition, the essential feature of the state of nature occupied by man was the law of nature, a moral law that Locke equated with God's will for mankind, the rightness of which man could perceive through the faculty of reason.

In the first proposition of his second treatise, he conceived of men as sharing a common origin in their creator even before they organized themselves into societies. "Thus the Law of Nature stands as an Eternal Rule to all Men, *Legislators* as well as others," he wrote. "The *Rules* that they make for other Mens Actions, must, as well as their own and other Mens Actions, be conformable to the Law of Nature, *i.e.* to the Will of God, of which that is a Declaration, and the *fundamental Law of Nature* being *the preservation of Mankind*, no Humane Sanction can be good, or valid against it."[6] This moral rather than political emphasis of Locke's theory of government, with its insistence on moral obligation, is the foundation of his system. What made Locke revolutionary was his denial of the theory that men are born into governmental arrangements and consequently obliged to obey those who may be governing by divine right, custom, or tradition. On the contrary, he said, it was individuals who created governments, and these governments functioned by the authority of a kind of "compact" or agreement involving the consent of the governed. Hence, a free people agreed to be governed but granted their governors responsibility in return for the security of their lives, liberty, and property. As long as government fulfilled those obligations, it permitted the government to stay in power.

Locke's liberalism also extended to the rights of individuals. Whereas previous political writers had viewed individuals as parts of corporate entities such as the church or the community, according to a common eighteenth-century interpretation Locke may be said to have viewed them as independent beings responsible for their fate and free to pursue their own self-interest without interference from government (though this interpretation has been challenged effectively).[7] When he explains that a law must have "the consent of society," then, he does not suggest that society must endorse each enactment but that there must exist a sense of historical solidarity by which the people express their approval. What is important about Locke's political thought is the way Locke emphasizes the state's responsibility to the community, a new way of viewing government that influenced more Whig attitudes as time went on and manifested itself in the language of both the parliamentary reform movement and the movement for independence in the American colonies.

From the fall of Walpole in 1742 to the introduction of Burke's economic reform bill in 1780, Jenyns kept his seat in Parliament and observed the changes taking place in political life as the populace clamored for more rights, the dissident Americans wrapped their protests in Lockean theory, and radicalism reached the very floor of the Commons. He shrank from the spectacle of the lower classes encroaching on what had been traditionally a gentleman's domain and withdrew from the primary concerns of the House until, after the violence that disrupted his first contested election in 1774, he lost his taste for political life. What were his attitudes to the business of government after such a lengthy career? In general, they were responses to the times—not abstract constitutional theories like those advanced by defenders of the Revolution but practical thoughts on the art of governing. In fact, he wrote, "Political authors, of all others, have the least understood their subject; which is not surprising, since authors are generally speculative men, and all knowledge of this kind entirely practical; wherefore he who has studied Aristotle and Plato, Grotius and Puffendorff, in his closet, will be less acquainted with the arts of governing than the meanest attorney, or the lowest alderman of the lowest corporation . . ." (2:229). We shall therefore examine his political writings in two groups: thoughts on the nature of government and political pamphlets.

The Nature of Government

Jenyns's thoughts on the nature of government appeared in three publications: the fifth letter of the *Free Inquiry* (1757), which placed "political evils" within the context of the evils afflicting mankind; a selection of political aphorisms that emerged here and there throughout "Reflections on Several Subjects," part of *Miscellaneous Pieces* (1761); and the seventh part of *Disquisitions on Several Subjects* (1782), "On Government and Civil Liberty," a condemnation of certain popular misrepresentations of the political principles of Locke. Two strong themes ran through all three. First, Jenyns viewed society not as an organism in a changing state but as a static hierarchy of classes in which the ascendant class protects and provides for its inferiors by virtue of its special fitness to govern. In effect, he was expressing a conservative acceptance of the status quo, since the gentry and the nobility had traditionally controlled the affairs of state by virtue of their superior birth and education. Second, he expressed an assumption that human failings handicapped men when they attempted to govern because of the inadequacies inherent in human nature.

The letter on "political evils" must be seen as part of the total metaphysic of the *Free Inquiry*, incorporating the theory that since man exists in the world as part of the work of a benevolent Creator, evil exists of necessity through the power of God, and society consequently consists of a system of subordination (see chapter 7). Within this framework, Jenyns offers some clear ideas about the nature of government, the nature of power, and the role of the individual, and he does so with the tone of the experienced, pragmatic politician. His thesis is that as long as the inadequacies of government are the fault of human nature, no change in the conduct of governmental affairs will take place without a reformation of manners. The nature of government he defines as power entrusted to "imperfect" and "vicious" creatures who exercise it over other imperfect and vicious creatures. This inevitably comes to pass because men lack the wisdom to pursue their common interests independently and therefore, as Locke had put it, submit to some kind of order to secure their lives and properties. But since everyone has a right to govern, it also leads to "ambition," "treachery," "violence," and "corruption." Self-interest, asserts Jenyns with his taste for scientific analogy, is the "great principle" operating in the world of politics just as attraction operates in the natural world, for men never submit to each other's authority out of a sense of long-term utility. They must be "beat or bribed" to obey. Governments therefore exist in order to allow one part of society to keep the other in subjection. They do not owe their origins (as the theorists had maintained) to patriarchal power, divine right, or democratic choice but to struggles of ambition and influence that eventually find their legitimacy in a policy.

According to Jenyns, the failure to understand this practical principle is the fundamental error of well-meaning "speculative politicians" or theorists bent on destroying governments and creating opposition to administrations when they do not find them perfect. They do not seem to realize, he adds, that imperfection is a part of human nature and that while it remains so, princes will seek ignoble ends just as the people will prefer immediate gratification of their self-interest to long-range benefits. Yet power must be entrusted somewhere, even though we recognize that no government can be administered without in some way "deceiving the people, oppressing the mean, indulging the great, corrupting the venal, opposing factions to each other, and temporising parties" (3:133–34). As Samuel Johnson pointed out, this did not amount to much more than an extension of Jenyns's discussion of moral evil, "polity" being "the conduct of immoral men in public affairs."[8] But as Jenyns goes on to say, the "evils" of government (taxes, standing armies, corruption in high places) give weight and popularity to the cause of those in opposition. While anyone may notice the inadequacies of government, it takes insight to see that men unconnected by self-interest will not act together any more than horses without bridles. Instead, they will "run riot, stop the wheels of government, and tear all the political machine to pieces" (3:135). The wise will accept the fact that these evils cannot be prevented and strive to prevent their excess. Nevertheless, the important question here, as Johnson realized, was how to determine when people should cease to accept the status quo and seek what they consider to be necessary changes.

Jenyns concludes by observing that politics is a "science" as reducible to certainty as mathematics. Though one man may act wisely, the behavior of the public is "constant and invariable." What, then, are the implications of such certainty for the exercise of political leadership? If virtue and benevolence are such rare qualities in the multitude, where is there to be found a statesman possessing these qualities and not conditioned by the ways of men? What follows is Jenyns's ironic portrait of the "*Great Man*," a creature of contradictions who possesses the qualities required by any successful politician:

he must be indefatigable in business, to fit him for the labours of his station, and at the same time fond of pleasures, to enable him to attach many to his interests, by a participation of their vices: he must be master of much artifice and knavery, his situation requiring him to employ, and be employed by, so many knaves; yet he must have some honesty, or those very knaves will be unwilling to trust him: he must be possessed of great magnanimity perpetually to confront surrounding enemies and impending dangers; yet of great meanness, to flatter those enemies, and suffer tamely continual injuries and abuses: he must be wise enough to conduct the great affairs of mankind with sagacity and success, and to acquire riches and honours for his reward; and at the same time foolish enough to think it worth a wise man's while to meddle with such affairs at all, and to accept of such imaginary rewards for real sufferings. (3:137–38)

Since this is the nature of the governor and of the governed, he concludes, all we can do to change the nature of politics is to reform our morals: people who act virtuously in their daily lives accomplish more than those who simply get rid of a bad governor, for the loss of a single politician is only a temporary relief at best.

"Reflections on Several Subjects" is Soame Jenyns's tabletalk, a collection of home truths, common sense, and philosophical insight on subjects such as religion, human nature, taste, and politics. These are usually aphoristic, and they reflect Jenyns's love of irony, paradox, and analogy. We learn, for example, "Whoever appears to have a great deal of cunning, must, in reality, have but very little; for if he had much, he would have enough to conceal it" (2:211) and that "Mankind live all in masquerade: he, therefore, who mixes with them unmasked is always ill received, and commonly abused by the whole assembly" (2:220). Most of them are arresting or striking in expression, particularly interesting as the thoughts of an experienced politician active at the beginning of the reign of George III and a conservative responding to the reforming tendency in British politics. For Jenyns viewed the rise of radicalism with alarm. His interest was the interest of the powerful landed elite, and he regarded the activities of reformers like John Wilkes as mere turbulence designed to create instability.

As a member of the landowning class who had traditionally run the affairs of the country, Jenyns supported the traditional prerogative of the House of Commons, most of whose members had gained their seats by means other than contested elections and who regarded themselves as patrons to their constituents. It is not surprising, then, to find him comparing the business of government to that of a nurse: to prevent those under its "care" from injuring themselves while taking abuse from them for any discomfort it might cause them. All government must be unpopular by its very nature, he argues, because it is nothing more than "a compulsion of individuals to act in such a manner for the support of society, as they are neither wise nor honest enough to do from the suggestions of their own heads and hearts" (2:224), something that is bound to run contrary to the inclinations of most people. On the other hand, admitting men into power by the force of "faction and opposition to power" weakens the state because it only incites more faction and opposition and incapacitates those who acquire power this way. Therefore, Jenyns does not consider the art of parliamentary confrontation to be a fruitful way to conduct business or a beneficial training ground for a leader, "it being as likely that a man should learn the science of government by the practice of disturbing it, as that he should acquire the skill of an architect by pulling down houses, or the trade of a glazier by breaking of windows" (2:224).

Jenyns could not imagine a constructive role for opposition except the role of a mischief-maker eager to gain power and preoccupied with bothering a stable administration doing its best for the good of the country. Clearly, he would not have favored Locke's dictum that the people hold within themselves the power to remove or alter a legislature acting contrary to the trust reposing in it, particularly one whose actions threaten the liberties and properties of the subject. He considered suggestions for doing away with prerogative and parliamentary influence as absurd and scorned the ideas of contemporary liberal thinkers, reducing those ideas generally to this, "that all government is an imposition of the few upon the many, which they ought perpetually to endeavour to shake off, and that the people ought to be governed by themselves only, that is, in other words, not to be governed at all" (2:227). He compared the mixture of learning and liberty in the hands of "the vulgar" to a cup of tea and brandy, both combinations being likely to find a mischievous use. Not surprisingly, he also distrusted the notion of "popularity" in politics and warned the leader secure in the sense of his own public appeal that "An able, honest, and wise minister, by various particular circumstances, may be popular for a time; but he is not very wise if he imagines that his popularity proceeds from any of these qualifications" (2:225). A minister who rises by his popularity will discover the same fate as a cat carried aloft by a paper kite: "while it lasts, it is all but scrambling and giddiness; and on the first change of the wind, or the breach of the pack-thread, down he tumbles."

The contemporary vogue for the word "liberty," one of the shibboleths of the radicals and a battle cry of the American colonists, irritated him again and again. The radicals took their cue from Locke, who had maintained that subjects must first be allowed to act like free men before they swear oaths of allegiance and submit to governments. When the Americans adopted this same attitude in 1776, Jenyns compared them to runaway horses in his comic ballad, writing,

> With bellies full of liberty,
>   But void of oats and hay;
> They both sneak back, their folly see,
>   And run no more away.

For him, the word suggested none of the Lockean connotations but threatened to undermine the established order by inciting the masses to pursue change without due consideration. "Liberty is a fine-sounding word," he cautioned, "but most of those who use it, mean nothing more by it than a liberty to oppress others, themselves uncontrouled by any superior authority" (2:213). To appreciate the weight of such a remark fully, one must also consider Jenyns's inherent acceptance of social distinctions.

As a country squire, he regarded businessmen, solicitors, and parsons as representatives of an order with whom he could associate easily only because they were aware of their subordinate places in the social system. It was no mean achievement for a member of the trading class to rise to a place among the landed gentry, let alone to acquire a seat in the House of Lords. The middle class did not fail through lack of effort, however, as he himself remarked in his scornful essay on aspiration in *World* no. 125, where he scoffed, "Were not the consequences of this ridiculous pride of the most destructive nature to the public, the scene would be really entertaining. Every tradesman is a merchant, every merchant is a gentleman, and every gentleman one of the nobless. We are a nation of gentry, *populus generosorum*: we have no such thing as common people amongst us: between vanity and gin, the species is utterly destroyed." Most Englishmen still inhabited self-contained villages. The country squire, as justice of the peace, exercised political and judicial authority and dominated local affairs as Jenyns himself did in Bottisham. Aware of the class differences between the landed interest and the trading interest, he instinctively felt their opposition to one another, and in one of his harshest observations remarked, "The landed interest of this nation, like the silly and defenceless sheep, in silence offers its throat to the butchery of every administration, and is eat up by every ravenous profession; while the trading interest, like the hungry and unmannerly hog, devours every thing, and if a finger is but laid upon it, the whole country is distracted with the outcry" (2:216). As the eighteenth century wore on, he found that nothing could be done to reverse this pattern of change.

If the foregoing comments by Soame Jenyns on political issues depend upon an appeal to practical experience rather than abstract thinking, the same is true of his essay "On Government and Civil Liberty," an attempt to refute Locke's *Second Treatise of Government*. This essay, thought the Whig apologist Richard Watson, bishop of Llandaff, was meant as an attack on his own sermon, *The Principles of the Revolution Vindicated* (1776), a diatribe against despotism arguing that the influence of the crown assisted ministers through the distribution or expectation of "private pensions, or the lucrative employments of public trust." If the Parliament, the nobility, or the king failed in their responsibilities, it concluded, the people had the right to take control of government into their own hands, to "lop off the rotten gangrened members" and to "purge the corruptions of the body politic" in any manner they saw fit.[9] Whether or not Jenyns had Watson's sermon in mind, the seventh disquisition was a more discursive and systematic presentation of his political philosophy than usual. In a previous disquisition, an elaboration of the analogy between things material and things intellectual, he had restated one of his essential precepts, reaffirming that self-interest was the primary force affecting government. In the same way that gravity affects large bodies or small, he had written, self-interest operates alike in the smallest parish or the most extensive empire. Men feel a direct benefit more acutely than the general prosperity of the country. Consequently, self-interest is the source of all human connections, a force that binds together families, cities, and nations and directs their labors:

"without its influence, arts and learning, trade and manufactures, would be at an end, and all government, like matter by infinite division, would be annihilated" (3:241). From this premise, he proceeded to counter the Lockean ideas being disseminated in the aftermath of the American Revolution, assuring his readers that to be refuted they required nothing more than to be stated fairly.

He first challenges with an irrelevant argument Locke's theory that all men are equal in the state of nature: that is, that all men born to the advantages of nature and the use of the same faculties should be equal "without Subordination or Subjection."[10] For Jenyns, such equality would be unrealistic and undesirable, and in his customary empirical manner he explores its implications by taking concrete examples. Some men are born healthy while others are riddled with disease; some are touched with genius and others with idiocy; some inherit fortunes and others live out their lives in obscurity. Neither do all possess an equal share of power, learning, and virtue, for not all are capable of acquiring it. Even if they did, not everyone would attain the same station in life. He asks, "must no man presume to be six feet high, because, perhaps, he was born of the same size as another, who is now but four? must no man assume power over another, because they were born equal, that is, because at birth they were both incapable of exercising any power whatever?" (3:259–60). Jenyns also questions the *continuance* of equality. Can men remain equal for very long, he asks? Calling attention to the inequalities imposed upon men in the course of their lives was no doubt a useful argument here, yet it did not consider the fact that the radicals were not seeking a redress from nature but equality of opportunity and the recognition of rights such as direct representation. At the time, while the propertied classes exercised more than an equal share of the voting power, the American colonists had already demonstrated that the pursuit of their own ideals could have far-reaching consequences. Jenyns could not have understood the full meaning of his words when he predicted that the concept of equality was one by which "all powers and principalities" were threatened with their overthrow.

Irritated by contemporary notions of "liberty," Jenyns

next assails the Lockean concept that all men are born free—that is, that all men are at liberty to "order their Actions, and dispose of their Possessions, and Persons as they think fit" within the bounds of the law of nature and without depending on the will of someone else.[11] In response to this, he reverts to his well-known weapons mockery and exaggeration to demonstrate what is beside the point, that the human condition is more naturally one of bondage than freedom. Confined for nine months to a "dark and sultry prison," he argues, man is no sooner set free than he is "bound hand and foot" and "fed upon bread and water." Once free of this, he abuses his liberty and requires the constraints of discipline, first by a nurse and then by a schoolmaster, who ignores his rights by confining him without charge, condemning him without cause, and whipping him without mercy. At length, he must submit to the authority of a civil government. Jenyns's rehearsal of the circumstances of the child are meant to show that the Creator never intended the individual to be independent and self-governing but to be brought up in a state of "subordination and government" so as to fit him for some future state. Here, his political and metaphysical ideas overlap, and with this appeal to the aims of Providence, he goes on to sound the warning that nothing disqualifies a person more in seeking a future reward than "a factious and turbulent disposition" and "an impatience of controul."

Anticipating the critics' charge of "ingenious ridicule," he nevertheless proceeds to his third point of contention: the idea that all government is derived from the people. With a wry smile, he facetiously concedes that this may be true when there are no people to govern but rejects what he calls the inference "usually" drawn from it, that the people have the right to resume it and administer it whenever they please. Reducing the argument to absurdity again, he concludes that this would leave nobody to be governed, for government is power, and if power is to rest in the hands of the people, who are "the people"? Jenyns answers that it is the nation under the direction of its "most respectable" members, persons of rank, property, wisdom, and experience—that is to say, those already possessed of advantages.

With characteristic mockery, he quickly adds that the reformers would replace such persons with those possessing no liberties or properties at all, "no public-spirit, but in the garrets of Grub-street; no reformation, but from the purlieus of St. Giles's; nor one Solon, or Lycurgus, but who is to emerge from the tin-mines of Cornwall, or the coal-pits of Newcastle" (3:265). By mentioning these last groups of indigents, Jenyns leaves no doubt about how ridiculous it would be to grant further power to the people. Grub Street and St. Giles's harbored the outlawed and the dispossessed; tinners and colliers joined other militant laborers in the food "riots" of the 1750s and 1760s as they seized large tracts of the countryside, requiring the government to call out the troops to restore order. Placing responsibility in the hands of such people would be absurd.

Next, Jenyns questions the principle of "compact" between governor and governed. Locke's theory of compact, as we have noted previously, depends so much on abstract argument that it makes itself vulnerable to well-known counterarguments. One of these Jenyns quickly grasps, and he brings it forward at the outset as he asserts the familiar irrelevant response that no such compact was ever literally agreed to and no such "natural independence" ever possessed. How, then, could it have been given up? Once again, Jenyns ignores a critical part of Locke's theory, the idea of tacit consent, which provides the governed not with a formal compact but with the *opportunity* to consent. Once they consent, wrote Locke, the people surrender all the power necessary to achieve the ends they united for and in return receive the protection of their rights.[12] Jenyns cannot conceive of a government that functions this way, and he argues, "Compact is repugnant to the very nature of government; whose essence is compulsion, and which originates always from necessity, and never from choice or compact; and it is the most egregious absurdity, to reason from the supposed rights of mankind in an imaginary state of nature, a state the most unnatural, because in such a state they never did or can subsist, or were ever designed for" (3:268). Government, then, is "natural" to man, but if each person is allowed the choice between "liberty and plunder" instead of "protection at the price of freedom," those who possess neither property nor principles will choose the former. Jenyns contrives this picture of society in ruin to emphasize the absurdity of building a political philosophy on speculation without the benefit of experience. Observing that people live naturally in societies, he concludes that government is a divine institution. The notion of "compact" implies a lack of government and therefore a transgression of the divine will.

Finally, Jenyns comes to Locke's proposal (later espoused by Bishop Watson) that the people hold the power to remove governments—as Jenyns construes it, "That no government ought to subsist any longer than it continues to be of equal advantage to the governed as to the governors" (3:271). This time, he oversimplifies, ignoring Locke's related concept of trusteeship. Locke had written, "all *Power given with trust* for the attaining an *end*, being limited by that end, whenever that *end* is manifestly neglected, or opposed, the *trust* must necessarily be *forfeited*, and the Power devolve into the hands of those that gave it, who may place it anew where they shall think best for their safety and security."[13] Locke was simply acknowledging here that while governments are entrusted with certain powers, they are obliged to employ them not in their own interest but on behalf of society. This idea commanded wide popular attention in the eighteenth century, and liberal doctrine of the same sort entered the jargon of parliamentary and social reformers. Yet it was so remote from anything Jenyns could conceive that he condemned such doctrine as anarchy. He further condemned its propagators as agitators ignorant of the realities of government and thirsty for power, equating their celebration of liberty with "an impatience of controul." Governments appear to be evil, he explains, because they constantly must deal with crime, venality, depravity, violence, avarice, ambition, profligacy, and idleness: "princes are made tyrants by the perverseness and disobedience of their subjects, and subjects become slaves from their incapacity to enjoy liberty" (3:276). Once bestowed, liberty must be circumscribed and adapted to the conditions of the people. To enjoy liberty is to allow oneself to be governed by equitable laws; to refuse to submit to one's government is to run the risk of suffering under the government of some foreign power.

As a whole, this essay is Jenyns's most systematic political statement, one that conveys a clear antagonism toward opposition in Parliament and toward efforts to resolve the difficulties of government by abstract thinking. He discounts the theories of Locke, but he is not totally at variance with those of Hobbes. Like Hobbes and Locke, he conceives of the state as a remedy for the evils arising out of man's natural condition rather than a natural institution, in the Aristotelian tradition, whose primary function is to promote the common good. Unlike Hobbes, Jenyns attributes to the state transcendent origins which governor and governed are obliged to acknowledge, yet for him it is Caesar who determines their mode of conduct, not God. The state is the result of the passions of men, particularly their self-interest; God only functions in the role of overriding judge. In a sense, his image of the structure of society is naturalistic, but this does not explain his authoritarianism. His authoritarian ideas of government did not spring completely from deduction. They were formed from his reactions to social and political change in England during a long parliamentary career outlasting war, civil unrest, and revolution. In the light of these events, he understood the importance of stability. What he has to say is dated and historically conditioned, like that of any practicing politician. Nevertheless, it does represent one strain of Whig thinking, the thinking of a man who had remained close to the institutions of power without wielding power himself and who depended on the good will of the crown and the government leader to keep his place and preserve his pension.

Political Pamphlets

The militia acts of the Restoration, derived from measures taken during the Interregnum, remained in force in England until the introduction of Pitt's militia bill in 1757. But ever since the establishment of a large standing army in the seventeenth century, politicians had regarded the military as a potential agent of the monarch, and they suspected increases in the strength of the army as attempts to extend the monarch's political influence as well. The military imbalance that existed at the middle of the eighteenth century, however, produced a feeling of national insecurity in England, and when the disasters at the beginning of the Seven Years' War brought Pitt into office, the time was appropriate for an act to establish a voluntary body of reservists who could be relied upon to keep the peace. The act that emerged was a regulatory act setting out the method for appointing both officers and men. It established oaths, penalties, payment (a shilling for officers; fourpence for private soldiers), allowances for families, the day and duration of exercises (Sundays not included), victualling ("Diet and Small Beer"), the furnishing of arms and accoutrements, and many other details.[14]

The Newcastle administration openly opposed the bill when it was introduced in 1756, and when they were replaced that year by the Devonshire-Pitt coalition, they continued to criticize it when it came up for debate again in the session of 1757. Although the bill successfully passed through the Commons, it met its most serious opposition in the Lords, where Hardwicke eloquently argued against it on constitutional grounds.[15] This legislation was important not only militarily but politically, for it was one of the last bills to limit royal patronage; and though it passed in the end, its opponents succeeded in revealing its serious drawbacks. Soame Jenyns's pamphlet *Short But Serious Reasons for a National Militia* (1757), undoubtedly a partisan venture undertaken in support of Hardwicke, chimed with the opposition's attack on the ideal of a citizen army composed mostly of farmers and men of property by ironically adducing six absurd reasons for approving of it, turning it into a subject of farce. The pamphlet was no dull recital of parliamentary debate, as the disarming title might suggest, but a witty piece of antiministry propaganda. With its comic detail and its sense of absurdity, it belongs to that body of satire, both in verse and in prose, that often pictured stout yeomen drilling in the fields under the gaze of their fellows before getting down to the more appealing business of playing cricket or relieving their parched throats at the local tavern.

Jenyns begins by brushing aside the anticipated objections, pointing out that with a few days' training the militia could grow as competent as the regulars had been during their recent reversals and, thereby, stifle the proposal to amalgamate the two forces in time of war. Their ration of small beer would inspire them as forcefully as gin inspires their professional counterparts, he continues, and drilling in a country churchyard would acquaint them better with death than drilling among the "gay scenes" of Hyde Park or St. James's. The lack of military knowledge would not handicap them either, for fighting only teaches men reasons for not fighting. He adduces positive reasons for a militia as well: securing liberty, property, and religion; strengthening the hands of government; reducing prices and promoting trade; boosting the population—all of which would be accomplished at a smaller expense. With these, he subjects the radicals and idealists to some straight-faced mockery. Liberties, he says as he takes up one of his favorite themes, make it possible for everyone to "think and write, and say and do whatever he pleases" and properties include whatever one can acquire. Since the arming of citizens would protect these precious assets from judges, juries, writs, jails, pillories, and officers of the law, this must strengthen government ("the sole right of the lowest of the people") because it provides people with arms and teaches them how to use them. The lowering of prices and the expansion of trade must follow naturally when the people can "take away" their provisions at a price they are best equipped to judge. Once prices fall, the cost of manufacturing would fall also, and more British products would be carried to foreign markets. Besides these economic benefits, the reader is also invited to consider the effects on population. Here is Jenyns in his characteristic burlesque stance:

figure to thyself all the handsomest young fellows in every county, each armed like the hero in a romance, drest, powdered, and toupeed by the reforming hand of a genteel serjeant; then turn thy eyes to the numerous groupe of fair spectators in Sunday gowns, and clean linen, who will not fail to attend so tempting a show; then if thou hast not lost all feeling both mental and corporeal, thou canst not doubt . . . that this will as infallibly be the cause of much procreation, and in a great measure repair the losses occasioned by our migrations to America, and the depredations of gin. (2:155-56)

Such procreation would more than compensate for any militiamen who might be accidentally killed while handling firearms.

To make the case complete, there is a little pleasant fun at the expense of the rustics in the form of a scheme to save public money. Observing that the bill before Parliament would allow the payment of sixpence to every man attending an exercise sober, Jenyns suggests a penalty of the same amount to be levied on those who attend drunk. This would bring the public purse nine times what it pays out, considering that no more than ten percent of those attending public gatherings in the counties is sober. The gentry also feel his playful irony. The bill assumed the gentry would refuse to serve without pay because their militia training would force them to quit their normal places of business; but Jenyns quickly shows how this drastically underestimated their public spirit, pointing to their readiness to act as justices and commissioners of taxes and their willingness to spend their time and fortunes trying to get elected to Parliament, "whence no possible advantage can accrue." In this manner, while ostensibly supporting the bill, Jenyns exposed it to his own particular form of genteel humor.

By comparison, Jenyns's next pamphlet, *The Objections to the Taxation of Our American Colonies, by the Legislature of Great Britain, Briefly Considered* (1765), was his most serious and controversial. So much has been written about the Stamp Act passed while Grenville was still in office, including an hour-by-hour rehearsal of its enactment and repeal, that it will be necessary to review only a few of the details here.[16] The Stamp Act was the British government's first attempt to draw significant revenue from America, and the total tax it envisaged was small. Although a stamp duty already existed as an accepted form of government revenue in Britain, the colonial Stamp Act was framed differently so as to meet conditions in the colonies and satisfy American susceptibilities. It provided for a wider range of duties calculated to distribute the burden more equitably, it stipulated that the funds raised were to remain in the colonies, and it left the administration to leading residents, not British officials. We may imagine the surprise of the Grenville administration, then, when the act met resistance from the commercial and intellectual elite in America, who turned the tax bill into a cause célèbre of parliamentary representation. What had seemed to be a reasonable and useful tax quickly became the symbol of oppression and a means for demonstrating the colonies' newfound maturity. As agents of the people, the colonials argued, governments require the people's consent before they impose taxes on them, and in this instance no consent had been given. While they recognized the authority of Parliament, they drew a distinction between taxation imposed for revenue and duties imposed for control. In the face of this unforeseen resistance, Parliament repealed the law in 1766, when the administration discovered its position to be untenable if only because it was unenforceable.

Predictably, Jenyns dismisses the Lockean language of the American advocates. He accepts taxation as he accepts government in general, as a necessary evil the people must tolerate or sink into anarchy. Brushing away all arguments to the contrary as either insolent or absurd, he makes a strictly legalistic interpretation of the issue based on his belief that Parliament, once it is convened, represents all British subjects and may act in any way it sees fit, for the people, at that point, play no part in the legislative process. As for the plea that "no Englishman is, or can be taxed, but by his own consent," he interprets this to mean the consent of the individual, his representative, or the elected majority. Drawing on recent English precedents, he wryly suggests that if no one could be taxed except by his own consent, no one would ever consent to it. Only a small proportion of the population possessed the franchise, and anyway the imposition of the cider tax had already shown that taxes could be imposed without the consent of the representatives. The Americans, he seemed to suggest, were scarcely at a greater disadvantage than their British relations.

Turning to the related issue of representation, Jenyns is willing to accept for the sake of argument the validity of the theory of "contract," aware that the Americans had invoked such authorities as Locke, Sidney, and Seldon to assert the claim that every Englishman is represented, whether or not he has the vote. "Why," he asks, "does not this imaginary representation extend to America, as well as over the whole island of Great Britain?" (2:193). It was James Otis who exposed the speciousness of this response, maintaining that until there was an extension of the franchise, one could just as easily prove Parliament represented all the people of the globe as prove it represented the Americans. But the Americans had also requested authority to levy taxes in their own legislatures and had viewed the denial of that authority as a loss of liberty. Such independent attitudes angered Jenyns, and he responded to this one with an outburst disrupting his otherwise calm, considered tone. "The liberty of an Englishman," he wrote, "is a phrase of so various a signification, having within these few years been used as a synonymous term for blasphemy, bawdy, treason, libels, strong beer, and cyder, that I shall not here presume to define its meaning; but I shall venture to assert what it cannot mean; that is, an exemption from taxes imposed by the authority of the parliament of Great Britain; nor is there any other charter, that ever pretended to grant such a privilege to any colony in America . . ." (2:194). The people are not always fit to judge what is a just or an unjust tax, he asserts, and since taxation does not fall equally upon all citizens, the whole system of taxation would end if all Englishmen protested Parliament's right to tax them.

Having defended Parliament's right to impose taxation, Jenyns next addresses himself to two particular criticisms of Parliament's action in the present crisis: the timing of the Stamp Act and the manner of its imposition. He appeals to the emotions of every Englishman who had watched the country drain its resources in an overseas war, leaving her colonies stronger than ever. Mindful of the assistance granted the colonies during his constant attendance at the Board of Trade, he asks sarcastically, "can there be a more proper time for this mother country to leave off feeding out of her own vitals, these children whom she has nursed up, than when they are arrived at such strength and maturity as to be well able to provide for themselves, and ought rather with filial duty to give some assistance to her distresses" (2:197–98). To the suggestion that local legislatures could impose the taxes equally as well under the authority of Parliament, he finds through the experience of dealing with colonists that they would not be willing to do so anyway. Again, he asks, "Have their assemblies shewn so much obedience to the orders of the Crown, that we could reasonably expect that they would immediately tax themselves on the arbitrary command of a minister? Would it be possible here to settle those quotas with justice, or would any one of the colonies submit to them, were they ever so just?" (2:198–99). If Parliament has the right to tax colonies, he submits, it should not be afraid to exercise that right. To introduce American representatives into Parliament would not alleviate the problem either, he adds sarcastically. With their great powers of speech "the sudden importation of so much eloquence at once" would be a threat to public safety. Leaning upon the authority of his own experience at the Board of Trade, he denies that the tax would impoverish the colonies and the commercial profits flowing back to Britain and concludes with a forceful appeal to members of all political stripes to support the bill. Jenyns must have taken some satisfaction from its subsequent passage, but as a pensioner he could not avoid reversing his position when the outcry forced its repeal in 1766, when he ironically had to vote with Bute against Grenville's motion to enforce it.[17]

When Jenyns turned his hand to pamphleteering the next time in *Thoughts on the Causes and Consequences of the Present High Price of Provisions* (1767), he was responding to the violence and social upheaval generated by the hunger "riots" of 1766–67. Faced with severe food shortages, militant laborers in the south of England threatened to upset public order in the spring and summer of 1766, and their violent protests brought out the military to protect market towns and country estates as the crisis developed.[18] These disorders expressed the discontent of poor workers victimized by seasonal and cyclical fluctuations in the economy, particularly by the high cost of living brought on by the conclusion of the Seven Years' War and by disappointing harvests.

At the risk of oversimplification, one could say that these protests arose out of a popular prejudice against the monopolism of farmers and against middlemen of the provisions trade, economic interests that were turned into scapegoats for a variety of social ills. Denunciations against middlemen flourished in newspapers, pamphlets, and correspondence in the 1760s, and they reached a peak during a period of scarcity and high prices in 1766–67. Faced with the possibility of public insurrection, the Chatham administration reenforced the prejudice by proclaiming laws against engrossers, regraters, and forestallers instead of taking other possible measures, such as prohibiting the export of grain and allowing the free importation of foreign supplies. As Walter J. Shelton has written, the government's action in proclaiming the statutes against engrossing, forestalling, and regrating revealed that it had failed to appreciate how the economy worked. It was inconsistent to allow large-scale grain exports while forbidding the practices necessary to assemble grain shipments destined for foreign markets and large urban centers like London.[19]

When Jenyns sat down to write this time, he abandoned his irony in favor of a considered, didactic approach to a practical economic problem. The high price of provisions and necessaries, he submits, is the result of "public poverty and private opulence," the "fatal disease" that has plagued the greatest of empires and eluded all remedies. Here, he was alluding to the conspicuous consumption of farmers adopting the style of a gentleman, a trend he had already attacked successfully in *World* no. 125, where he had commented, "Every commoner of distinction is impatient for a peerage, and treads hard upon the heels of quality in dress, equipage and expences of every kind. The nobility, who can aim no higher, plunge themselves into debt and dependance, to preserve their rank; and are even there quickly overtaken by their unmerciful pursuers." More particularly, he was responding to the construction placed upon the public turmoil by writers in the newspapers, who were blaming the calamity on monopolizers, regraters, forestallers, and engrossers, encouraged, in turn, by politicians insensitive to the complaints of the people. In response to these writers,

Jenyns sets out to establish what he calls the "true causes" issuing from two other sources: the immense national debt and the increase of private affluence.

What follows, then, is a lesson in the management of currency and taxation. Jenyns attempts to show how every citizen was in effect paying for the immense borrowings undertaken by the government to fight the Seven Years' War in paying his taxes and how the funding of the debt was creating wealth for individuals in forcing more cash to circulate, thereby encouraging trade and commerce both at home and abroad. He notices two effects of the perceived increase in affluence: with more money circulating, the value of money decreases; with increased purchasing, people produce scarcity by their luxurious style of living and their increased expectations. He is therefore at pains to account for high prices without blaming "forestallers, regraters, engrossers, monopolizers, higlers, badgers, bounties, postchaises, turnpike-roads, enlarging of farms and the extension of the metropolis," the established targets of contemporary writers, for the simple reason that products cannot become costly in a poor country. In short, people cannot charge high prices where there is no money to be found.

In summing up, he accepts high prices as a natural phenomenon in any country engaged in war or successful commerce because there will inevitably be high taxes and large incomes, but he adds that the devaluation of money affects people differently. While the trader and the merchant profit, those on fixed incomes, like the laborer and the landowner, are the last to feel the effects of cheap money. What is the solution? The administration should cease turning middlemen into outlaws and very gradually reduce the national debt without incurring any further liabilities: that is to say, by discouraging new commercial enterprises, resisting the settlement of new colonies financed by parliamentary estimates, and staying out of new wars. By not stimulating the economy further, these measures would reduce the expectations of the people and avoid the disappointment that would lead to further violence.

Jenyns's next pamphlet appeared at the end of three turbulent years dominated by the reforming agitations of John

Wilkes, the radical whose activities found support and publicity in the anonymous letters of "Junius." *A Scheme for the Coalition of Parties* (1772) responded to the well-known "discontents" that occurred when Parliament refused to seat Wilkes in 1769 (even after he had been elected M.P. for Middlesex four times) and finally declared his nearest rival the winner. At the time, there was widespread economic distress in London, and the potentially violent crowds that gathered looked to Wilkes as a symbol of revolt against what they perceived to be social injustice. The Wilkes affair clearly delighted the opposition members when it embarrassed the Grafton-North administration over the sensitive issue of whether the House of Commons possessed the right to declare a candidate elected on a minority vote. Wilkes was indeed seen by conservatives as a disreputable character, but the Rockingham opposition seized the opportunity provided by the Wilkes affair to attack what they considered to be the power and influence of the crown. By seeking a union of opposition factions on principle alone, it set out to destroy the perceived "Court party" in power. The pamphlet purported to respond to the announcement that "a certain able politician" would soon be making public a scheme for the coalition of parties. In the absence of any observable principle separating the groups ("they are neither Whigs nor Tories, Monarchy-men nor Republicans, High-church nor Low-church, Hanoverians nor Jacobites") it concluded that the differences between them were nothing more than "an outrageous contest for power and profit" and set out to expose with facetiousness the turbulence maintained by factions.

Without mentioning any name except the Society of Supporters of the Bill of Rights, the group formed in 1769 to give financial and political support to Wilkes, Jenyns proceeds to make his argument a *reductio ad absurdum* by introducing a scheme to restore order to parliamentary politics by chance alone. Aware that the radicals proposed the election of annual parliaments, he goes a step further and suggests an annual administration of thirty peers and a hundred members of the Commons who would take possession of the great offices of state year by year by drawing the names from a sealed box. This would promote two main benefits: it would bring political upheaval to an end and allow the "much-sought-for coalition" to fall into place. As a means of drawing attention to the current instability and throwing into relief the claims of the radicals, Jenyns goes on to mention how such a proposal would benefit the various segments of society. While it would relieve the king of one of his choicest powers, he says, it would also relieve him of "the disagreeable necessity of preferring knaves for their intrigues, profligates for their abilities, and fools for their connexions" and save him the trouble of hearing petitions from those who have not received appointments. Ministers would then be able to devote their energies to the business of government for a whole year without being bothered by the petty problems that take up their time: unable to promise anything for the future, they would not need to go back on their word. Turning to the opposition, the main target of the pamphlet, he finds that under the proposed system they would be relieved of their barren occupation. Having no single ministry against which to exert themselves, "they will therefore no longer be obliged to toil and sweat, whole days and nights, in supporting questions, which they disapprove: and motions, which they neither expect nor wish to carry; they will no more be obliged to expend their own fortunes in forming clubs, cementing factions, fomenting tumults, and purchasing petitions, on the bare possibility of being some time or other reimbursed by the public" (2:264–65). All of this would certainly improve the state of the country, he predicts, by eliminating the distressing discontents of the past fifty years. What all of this amounted to was a characteristically amusing *jeu d'esprit* but an inconsiderable contribution to the debate as a whole.

The reform movement that shook Parliament in the 1770s bewildered Jenyns. He was outraged at having to contest an election in 1774, and when he retired in 1780 after the introduction of Burke's economic reform bill, he refused to accept the fundamental changes already taking place in British politics. When he had entered Parliament in 1741, few of his fellow members were "professional politicians," as we understand the term today, but rather a selection of men from the upper classes who saw it as their duty to represent the country at large rather than their own constituents in particular. From time to time, they gathered to vote supplies and to ensure that the crown did not engross too much executive power. During Jenyns's career the clamor for parliamentary reform grew steadily louder. But while radicals embraced parliamentary reform as the chief means of preserving personal liberties and safeguarding the constitution from the court, they could not agree on the extent of such measures as annual parliaments, the secret ballot, or the redistribution of seats from the rotten boroughs to the larger urban centers. Jenyns stiffened against such measures. Clinging to his conservative view, he published in 1784 his final pamphlet, *Thoughts on a Parliamentary Reform*,[20] a judgment on political change ridiculing the cherished beliefs of the reformers with a burlesque performance portraying the poor, the uneducated, and the dispossessed handling the reins of power.

This time, Jenyns confines himself specifically to the concept of an independent Parliament as a cure for the political ailments of the nation as well as to the means of achieving such a Parliament and the possible effects of it. First, he dismisses as impracticable such measures as annual parliaments, voting by ballot, annihilating corrupt boroughs, and changing the qualifications required of electors, imagining only the possibility of the multitude "let loose" on election day in reaching the conclusion that "such a scene of confusion, of drunkenness and riot, of rapine, murder, and conflagration" would be shockingly horrible. Groups such as the gentry, the town corporations, and the freemen of London would never allow themselves to vote with them on an equal footing, he assures his readers, and even the people themselves would learn that nothing had been gained when they realized that bribery and corruption would have to come to an end. It would not even improve the quality of the members, who would act in the same manner as the present ones, splitting up into factions and looking after their own interests. As for the effects of an independent Parliament ("a parliament in which the majority would oppose any administration"), Jenyns is assured it could never transact business while men act naturally out of self-interest and not on the merits of the case. Something such as the leadership of a powerful minister must unite them, he says: "An independent House of Commons is no part of the English constitution, the excellence of which consists in being composed of three powers, mutually dependent on each other: of these, if any one was to become independent of the other two, it must engross the whole power to itself, and the form of our government would be immediately changed" (2:245–46). An assembly cannot operate without influence, he finds, something quite distinct from corruption. He himself was an example of how a member could operate satisfactorily within the present system, and he was emphasizing instead the distinction between voting for a minister and entering Parliament in pursuit of power, obstructing and distressing the administration until it is obtained. The present system may not satisfy the needs of everyone, he admits, but it is better to tolerate its flaws and to be thankful for the benefits secured under it than to dismantle it in favor of a system whose flaws cannot be foreseen. It was a plea for stability by a government pensioner unequivocally loyal to the crown at a time when the value of such loyalty was being questioned.

Jenyns wrote only one other pamphlet, which he did not send to the press.[21] This time, he supported the economic reforms inaugurated by the younger Pitt after the election of 1784 and approved of the sinking fund created to contribute a million pounds a year to reducing the national debt. The plan had appealed to Jenyns, and in "Thoughts on the National Debt" he praised the measure so warmly as to predict that "no plan more efficacious can be devised." If it could "pare away insensibly" part of the debt each year, it would not distress the public or its creditors. Undoubtedly, he did not publish the pamphlet because it advanced the same argument as the one on the high price of provisions. Here, Jenyns repeated his observation that large public loans had put money in people's pockets, fostering high expectations and driving up prices, and once again he ridiculed the newly affluent while he bemoaned the fate of the country gentry.

In praising the undertaking to reduce the national debt, the pamphlet does in fact lecture the reader on the perils of term financing, beginning by dismissing the "political and theological prophets" who have misrepresented the nature of the debt, particularly by comparing public debt to private debt. Unlike an individual who contracts a private debt, Jenyns argues, the public is not obliged to repay a debt it owes itself. Paradoxically, the public is enriched by what it owes, whereas a private debtor enriches himself when his debts are discharged. Once again, he points out that the increased affluence enjoyed in Britain was being derived directly from the existence of the national debt:

> Let us now take a view of the astonishing contrast of our present opulence and luxury, which has gradually grown up and kept pace with our debt. The landed gentleman, fitted by education for some honourable and lucrative profession, is no longer to be found amidst the dirt and penury of the country, but appears with affluence and dignity in the character of a general or admiral, a judge or a bishop; our commerce is extended, and our manufactures improved; our lands are better cultivated, and our people in every rank of life better fed, clothed, and lodged, than in any former period. (2:290)

To support this claim, he then takes the hypothetical case of an administration fitting out and victualling a fleet that will require a million pounds to finance. To defray the annual interest of five percent, Parliament levies taxes, but before long the borrowed funds are issued to sailors, tradesmen, and artificers and subsequently diffused throughout the other occupations and professions. The wealth of the nation as a whole cannot thus be impaired, for the nation borrows as a corporate body and lends as a society of individuals. The *circulation* of money creates affluence when it provides the opportunity to spend and to borrow again. The increase of money diminishes its value: prices rise, and the burden falls unevenly on the various ranks of society.

Generally speaking, these pamphlets are consistent with Jenyns's political philosophy. They imply a conservative attitude toward the role of the crown and Parliament, supporting virtual representation in Parliament for all the king's subjects, the continuance of the current parliamentary system of influence, and the value of the British constitution as it stood. In the field of economics, they advocate traditionally static remedies for trade and commerce, remedies that would be made obsolete by Adam Smith's *Wealth of Nations* (1776).

Chapter Six
Philosophical and Religious Prose
The New Science and Natural Religion

The eighteenth century marks an important stage in the history of religious controversy, a stage at which the direction of English theology changed fundamentally. No one was thrown into prison for holding unorthodox beliefs; no churches were desecrated; no heads were lopped off. Yet for a time there continued a prolonged battle of wits that left men's attitudes toward belief and the practice of the religious life altered forever. Little by little, the scientific discoveries of Galileo and Newton had altered the medieval world picture of the universe; but although these were scientific discoveries, they could not avoid also calling into question the established ecclesiastical interpretation of a universe ruled by a benevolent God by substituting a new view of a tiny planet occupied by man in the vast, unimagined regions of space. Previously, men's thinking about the world around them had existed within the context of a monarchical model constructed from a literal interpretation of the Bible, from Greek philosophy, and from medieval Scholasticism. Toward the end of the seventeenth century, however, a new mechanical concept of the universe began to penetrate English theological life. Since that time, it could be said that Christian apologetic has preoccupied itself with the task of bringing religious and scientific assertions into some kind of satisfactory relationship.[1]

The New Science encouraged mankind to eschew authority and tradition and to embrace reason as a safe guide to knowing the natural world. In response to this challenge, "natural religion" became the central feature of what might be called the British "enlightenment," not as a system of beliefs antagonistic to Christianity but as a habit of mind assuming reason to be supreme in the understanding of religious matters. The fundamental argument of natural religion was the "design argument," one that inferred God's existence from the data supplied by science. Thus, if God's handiwork could be seen by analogy to be manifested in the detail and pattern of nature, reasoning could also be seen as a force binding both science and theology in a common method. There was nothing heretical about this. Rationalist thinkers would certainly not have described themselves as atheists but as believers who continued to partake of the sacraments and sing the well-known hymn of Joseph Addison that gives us these lines:

> What though in solemn silence, all
> Move round the dark terrestrial ball?
> What though, nor real voice nor sound
> Amid their radiant orbs be found?
> In reason's ear they all rejoice,
> And utter forth a glorious voice,
> For ever singing as they shine,
> "The hand that made us is divine."[2]

As natural religion continued to infiltrate speculative thought, it could not also help question the teachings of revelation presented in the Scriptures. According to the Bible, man was a fallen creature born in sin and in need of the benefit of God's grace. The orthodox religious life rejected the things of this world and encouraged the practice of asceticism. But the doctrine of original sin as an explanation of the ills inherent in the world was now being seriously questioned as the world was being interpreted as the handiwork of God. Philosophers seeking other ways to explain religious belief shifted the cause and origin of evil elsewhere: they had to recognize and prove the "necessity" of the source of evil in the eyes of reason.

Central to the history of natural theology in a scientific age are the claims of the deists, an assortment of writers who, without constituting an organized movement, first raised the problems implied by natural theology and set Christian apologists on the defensive. What followed was a prolonged conflict between deistic and orthodox thinkers that continued throughout the eighteenth century in a spirit of polite disputation. Throughout the many stages of this conflict, the deists were not content merely to provide theoretical objections to revelation. They also attempted to discredit it on historical grounds. Once they had called the literal infallibility of the Bible into question, the conflict broke forth, and the church responded by appealing to its traditional defenses, emphasizing the uniqueness of the life of Christ and the distinctive experience of the early Christians. Fundamental to its argument were the "evidences" to be adduced from the life of Christ as manifested in the Bible through the witness of the early church as well as the implications of prophecy and miracle. Did these add anything to the conclusions of natural religion or merely confirm them? The answer to this question was crucial to the defenders of revealed religion, who recognized that their defense must somehow satisfy the demands of reason. In the later decades of the eighteenth century, however, this preoccupation with reason diminished as abstract theological speculation grew increasingly dissatisfying and unfashionable. At that time, apologists for Christianity turned to defending their religion by emphasizing the credibility of its sources and the utility of its ethics, *internal* marks of its divinity that found their fullest expression in the works of William Paley.

A distinctively rationalist cast of religious thought dominated the intellectual environment in which Soame Jenyns grew up. Although he received an orthodox Christian upbringing at the hands of his mother and two clerical tutors and drank in the Anglicanism of St. John's College, Cambridge, we should not be surprised by his reflections in 1748:

> I would by no means church or king destroy,
> And yet the doctrines, taught me when a boy
> By CRAB the curate, now seem wond'rous odd,
> That either came immediately from God:
> (1:91)

nor is it surprising that he embraced the fashionable doctrine of benevolence in "An Essay on Virtue," railed against the negativeness of Christian ethics, and predicted that once it was elminated, "How soon must reason o'er the world prevail, / And error, fraud, and superstition fail!" (1:60). In his maturer years, while some observers thought Jenyns shrugged off the orthodoxy of his upbringing, nowhere did he profess to be an unbeliever, not even in *A Free Inquiry into the Nature and Origin of Evil*, where he adapted the tenets of "optimism" to his own use without casting doubt on revelation. Moved by the spirit of the time, he preferred to modify orthodoxy from within. In the preface to the third edition of the *Free Inquiry*, he replied to his critics by emphasizing that he had had no intention of undermining the foundations of Christianity but believed the spirit of free enquiry did more good than "the enlisting legions under that denomination whose immoveable faith proceeds only from their ignorance; that is, who believing without any reason, can possibly have no reason for doubting" (3:21). Here he was constrained to declare his Christian faith, framing his intentions in the language of the age as he set out to show the "excellence" and "credibility" of Christian revelation, to reconcile its "abstruse doctrines" with reason, and to answer objections to its authority drawn from its "imperfections and abuses." In fact, Jenyns praised the very tenets of Christianity that he would later admire in *A View of the Internal Evidence of the Christian Religion*—"its internal excellence, the reasonableness of its morality, the sublimity of its theology, that it alone has fixed the right criterion of virtue, alone discovered the magnanimity of forgiveness" (3:144). So bold a statement casts doubt upon the facile claim of his critics that a so-called "conversion" took place between the writing of these two volumes.

In the eyes of some, Jenyns's writings clearly indicated that he had returned to the fold after a prolonged absence. Toward the end of Jenyns's life, Hannah More wrote to her sister, "Whatever scepticism he might once have been charged with, I believe him now to be a real believer: the doubts entertained by some persons of his sincerity, appear in his late work on the internal evidence of Christianity to be quite unfounded."[3] Paley judged him to be an "acute observer of human nature" and a "sincere convert to Christianity."[4] Even though evangelical writers of the early nineteenth century have seized upon his life as an example of one who strayed from orthodoxy and later found true religion,[5] there is nothing to indicate that Jenyns's conviction or his behavior altered dramatically. His contemporaries found him to be uniformly pleasant and even-tempered, mild-mannered, reflective, and benevolent. His travel journal records his regular attendance at church services even while on tour, and his companion Charles Nalson Cole attests to his "strict" and "constant" attention to his religious duties both publicly and privately, assuring us that he professed the "greatest veneration" for the Church of England as an institution.[6] At no time did he claim to be anything other than a Christian, even as he adopted the fashionable mode of expression of natural religion, just as Pope, a professed Roman Catholic, adopted it in his *Essay on Man*. While it is easy to label someone writing this way a "deist," it should also be remembered that the term is not precise. As Professor Mack has pointed out in his introduction to the *Essay on Man*, it could cover a range of attitudes from the outright rejection of Christianity to a mild skepticism about the literal truth of the Old Testament, much as the term "Tory" could be applied to a country gentleman or a Whig out of favor.[7] Like Pope, Jenyns was attracted to natural theology and wished to be identified with it without unequivocally opposing traditional Christian doctrines based on revelation. At times he contradicts himself and at times he takes unorthodox theories too seriously, but at heart he remains a Christian speaking the language of his age.

The *Free Inquiry* and Johnson's Review

Perhaps the most vexing problem in religious thought throughout the centuries has been how to reconcile the presence of evil in the world with the existence of an omnipotent and benevolent God. Since the days of the early church, the church fathers have been faced with the task of defending divine justice and righteousness in the face of evil, and the whole subject comprising the problem and its resolution has come to be known as "theodicy." It was St. Augustine who shaped Christian thought on the subject, and although the subsequent debate has been a complex one, Augustine's solution has remained influential. Augustine based his solution on what he called the principle of "plenitude," the principle that the universe exemplifies every possible kind of existence, the lower and the higher, the imperfect and the perfect. In the light of this principle, evil may thus be defined as a lack of good or the service of a greater good that we see but in part. The age of natural religion was also the great age of theodicy. The problem of evil preoccupied rationalist thinkers, who brought to its ultimate conclusion the concept of evil as something serving a greater good. The universe, they said, could certainly be seen to be evil in many ways, but it was the best universe possible given the benevolence and omnipotence of God. This theory of "optimism" received prominence in William King's *Essay on the Origin of Evil*, which first appeared in Latin in 1702 and probably inspired Pope's *Essay on Man*. On the Continent, it found its most influential expression in Leibniz's *Théodicée* (1710). Jenyns's *Free Inquiry* should therefore be regarded as one of numerous English theodicies adopting the notion that in spite of the presence of evil, this is indeed the best of all possible worlds, a notion calling forth as many critics as supporters.[8]

In the *Free Inquiry*, Jenyns based his argument on a set of ideas owing their genesis to Plato and Aristotle and their systematization to the Neoplatonists: the principle of plenitude and the conception of the created universe as a "scale of being."[9] Plenitude assumes that the whole range of conceivable beings is exemplified in the universe and that no potentiality can remain unfulfilled. Creation was assumed to be as great as the possibility of existence and commensurate with the capacity of an inexhaustible source or creator. From this, the principle of "continuity" was deduced. This principle asserted that if there was a theoretically possible type between two given natural species, that type must be realized. In addition, the idea that all created beings are arranged in a graded "scale" was also widely accepted in the eighteenth century. Thus, the conception of the universe as a scale of being, with its underlying principles of plenitude, continuity, and gradation, was widely diffused, and its presence served as a basis for Jenyns's thought. In effect, Jenyns's interpretation of it was already familiar in many ways, particularly the assumption that in a perfect whole there are parts that are only *apparently* imperfect or imperfect without reference to the whole. To apply this concept to the natural world, one would then conclude that a perfect universe created by an omnipotent creator must allow all possible things (including evil) and that evil is only apparent. The *Free Inquiry* is one of the most readable expressions of this line of thought if not the most consistent. Full of the cant of natural religion and couched in an epistolary style, it would have found favor with the general reader. But if Jenyns attracted readers with his ease of expression, he sometimes abandoned his empiricism for fancy and arrived at his conclusions too quickly.

By dividing his treatise into six "letters" addressed to a supposed correspondent, Jenyns proceeds to lay out the philosophical foundations in the first three letters and to discuss the implications for human behavior in the last three. His purpose is a practical one. An understanding of the problem, he explains, provides a basis for a "rational system of ethicks." By taking *a priori* the benevolence of the Creator, he seeks to reconcile that benevolence with the misery and suffering we experience. Upon the solution to the whole problem, he suggests, all human virtue depends. An understanding of it will confirm the nature of virtue and man's obligation to pursue it. Sweeping away historical explanations of the nature of evil—the Manichaean system of two first causes, the loss of a golden age or paradisaical state, the abuse of free will—he invokes the principle of plenitude to show how certain evils can exist in a world created by a benevolent God. His answer to the apparent paradox is that omnipotence can only "effect all possible things," and that it would have been impossible to create a world exclusive of evil. Evils exist "of necessity": according to the principle of plenitude (which assumes that we do not ourselves perceive all possibilities) their prevention would have entailed the loss of superior good or the permission of greater evil. Thus, he concludes that evil is consistent with God's power and goodness.

The concept of a scale of being "descending by insensible degrees from infinite perfection to absolute nothing" does not appear until the second letter, where Jenyns employs it to explain the absence of comparative good in beings that are necessarily inferior to other beings. Every system, he explains, consists of subordinate parts: what *appear* to be imperfections are really blessings extending to an inferior degree. Since gradation is also a feature of human society, he consequently makes a deduction justifying inequality and approving of a static society in which everyone is to know his place and keep it. This was one of Jenyns's characteristically imaginative leaps, and to justify it he confidently asserts that though all cannot be equally happy, God has made all beings as happy as their "respective situations" permit. What exactly does this mean? The answer, while it recognizes the reality of inequality, brings forward some questionable instances. He tells us that poverty is compensated by more hopes and by the relish of small enjoyments, the want of taste by common sense, sickness by trifling gratifications and the return of health, and madness by a pleasure "which none but madmen know." Most striking of all is the rationalization that ignorance is good for the poor. "Ignorance," he writes, "or the want of knowledge and literature, the appointed lot of all born to poverty, and the drudgeries of life, is the only opiate capable of infusing that insensibility which can enable them to endure the miseries of the one, and the fatigues of the other. It is a cordial administered by the gracious hand of providence; of which they ought never to be deprived by an ill-judged and improper education" (3:49–50). While such a recommendation would never be applauded by the poor, it is perfectly consistent with Jenyns's overall view of the universe as a "well-regulated family" in which each member enjoys the privileges of his place and, by so doing, contributes to the happiness of the whole by maintaining a system of subordination.

Having laid the foundation of his argument, in the third letter Jenyns accounts for the existence of "natural evils" (poverty, labor, inquietudes of mind, pain, and death) with a standard optimistic justification that had been put memorably in these lines of Pope:

> All Nature is but Art, unknown to thee;
> All Chance, Direction, which thou canst not see;
> All Discord, Harmony, not understood;
> All partial Evil, universal Good:
> And, spite of Pride, in erring Reason's spite,
> One truth is clear, "Whatever IS, is RIGHT."[10]

This expressed a common theme of eighteenth-century optimists, who occupied themselves with demonstrating that even though evils exist, they exist of necessity. They do exist in this world, they insisted, but any other world capable of existence would be even worse. The *Free Inquiry* thus accords with eighteenth-century optimism by offering a comprehensive solution to the problem while maintaining a reasoned acquiescence in the inherent imperfections of a perfect world, imperfections that could not have been prevented without the loss of a greater good or the admission of greater evils. Jenyns himself even goes as far as to suggest that there is something in the "abstract nature" of pain conducive to pleasure and that even though we are unable to perceive what it is, it is necessary to human happiness. With another imaginative leap, he offers by analogy the solution that our sufferings may be inflicted by superior beings who may exist in the vast scale of things, interfering with men's lives as men interfere with the lives of animals. If we find this difficult to accept, he suggests, we should be assured that the justice of the Creator will balance our happiness or misery equitably in some future state. To establish that such a state exists, he invokes the doctrine of the transmigration of souls as one that seems the "most rational" and "most consistent" with God's wisdom and goodness. (In the "Essay on Virtue" he had already put this vividly and in *World* no. 163 had expounded the Pythagorean theory of transmigration in some detail.) He would return to this doctrine again in *Disquisitions on Several Subjects*. For the present, it served to introduce a hint of hope into a world where evil could not apparently be avoided.

Jenyns now proceeds to what he considers the important ethical consequences of the foregoing in his discussion of moral evil, political evils, and religious evils. In the light of the foregoing speculations, he had concluded that the operation of the universe (which we know only in part) is somehow predetermined and that we should therefore quietly submit to the evils we encounter, which exist of necessity. Turning to the known world, he then transfers this conclusion by analogy to human affairs and attempts to demonstrate how immorality, corrupt government, and an imperfect religion exist of necessity as well. To justify it, he conceives of the world as a "school of probation and education" where human beings may improve or debase themselves. This was a concept he found useful as a metaphysician. In the "Essay on Virtue," he termed the world a "sportive nursery" provided by a benevolent God; in *A View of the Internal Evidence* it became "the state of probation for the kingdom of heaven"; and in Disquisition III (on a preexistent state) he described it as a "place of punishment as well as probation; a prison, or house of correction" to which we are committed during our lifetime. In a world conceived this way, Jenyns defines moral good and evil as "the production of the natural," acts to be judged in terms of their consequences. If an action produces good, it is virtue; if it produces evil, it is vice. Our tendency to be moral or immoral, therefore, depends on our natures, especially on our "appetites," our "vanity," our "compassion," our "bounty," and our fears for self-preservation.

The *Free Inquiry* differs from the more overtly orthodox theodicies of the eighteenth century in rejecting the doctrine that moral evil originates in the abuse of free will. A just and beneficent creator would never have admitted moral evil into creation, Jenyns suggests, unless that evil offered some collateral benefit. If misery could not have been excluded, it was something to be endured by a creature such as man, a creature inclined to bring suffering upon himself yet possessed of the reason and free will required to escape it. Having demonstrated to his own satisfaction that "natural evil" is a product of necessity, he now concludes that moral evil is equally consistent with divine goodness; and from here it is an easy step to show that an inferior creature such as man is also necessarily exposed to political and religious evils. Governments, we are told, are founded on either force or interest and supported by the compulsion and corruption that produce evils. God cannot prevent them, says Jenyns, but man can do so by diminishing the moral evil from which they are derived: that is, by enduring them for the time being and working for a reformation of manners. Such a view was consistent with the abstract nature of optimism. For those seeking to justify their prerogatives and privileges, it was a handy guide to behavior. While it advocated morality, it also discouraged any alteration in the social system. As for the barbarous and obscene acts carried out in the name of religion, Jenyns explains that it is impracticable to give a perfect religion to an imperfect creature. Natural religion cannot be fully comprehended by a reason that is unstable and limited; revealed religion is wasted on a creature incapable of comprehending its mysteries.

The *Free Inquiry* was ethical rather than metaphysical in its emphasis, and its line of argument confined it within a narrow framework. It confined its consideration of evil to what was considered appropriate to man's position in the great chain of being, and it found that the good and evil he experiences exist to the degree we would expect from a creator with infinite benevolence and power. While such a thoroughly speculative treatment of the subject ignored certain realities of life as it was being lived, it did attract a good deal of attention, most notably from Samuel Johnson, whose review in the *Literary Magazine* mustered so much vehemence that it kept the memory of the *Free Inquiry* alive long after controversy over the problem of evil had shifted to other ground. In 1757, Johnson's review was not the most thorough analysis. Divines such as Richard Shepherd and Caleb Fleming reviewed the work more systematically. But Johnson went to the heart of the matter. He was concerning himself mainly with the philosophical foundations laid in the first three letters, which provided him with an opportunity to dispatch the doctrines he so disapproved of in his life of Pope. It will be useful to digress here and to consider those objections briefly.

Johnson scholars have called attention to the way Johnson ridiculed Jenyns as a Whig placeman and published his findings in a magazine with a distinctly political stance. But Johnson did not so much set out to embarrass the government as to expose the absurdity and contradiction of a widely accepted idea. Johnson the empiricist was at work here, quick to show that a system of ethics erected on a Platonic metaphysic must produce no other consequence than to "perplex the scrupulous, and to shake the weak, to encourage impious presumption, or stimulate idle curiosity."[11] While other critics advanced the orthodox theological position, Johnson commanded the reader's attention not only for the force and satiric quality of his thundering periods but, like his criticism of the dramatic unities in the history of literary criticism, for the importance of his analysis in the whole history of optimism.[12] Johnson was no metaphysician. He did not allow himself to become entangled in conjecture about the unknown, especially the teleological arguments advanced by Jenyns. Rather, Johnson the empiricist was showing that such arguments were not related to experience. "This author and *Pope* perhaps never saw the miseries which they imagine thus easy to be born," he suggested. Later, he continued sarcastically, "When this author presumes to speak of the universe, I would advise him a little to distrust his own faculties, however large and comprehensive." Still later, with reference to Jenyns's presumed lack of independence as a Whig placeman, he chided, "Surely a man who seems not completely master of his own opinion, should have spoken more cautiously of omnipotence, nor have presumed to say what it could perform, or what it could prevent."[13] Nevertheless, although rebukes such as these are scattered throughout the review, Johnson the moralist was primarily interested in expressing his indignation about the implications of Jenyns's ideas for human behavior. By not recognizing the proper distinction between good and evil, concluded Johnson, Jenyns was leading in the opposite direction, to a breakdown of ethics. Lacking the scope on this occasion to lay out a thorough orthodox interpretation of his own, Johnson was satisfied to expose frivolous logic and dismiss contradiction.

Johnson's review is interesting, then, not just as a contemporary assessment of Jenyns as a would-be empiricist but as a statement disposing of a theory "ready to fall to pieces" of itself. The theory of a "chain" of being curtails freedom of choice to the individual, Johnson notices, yet it asserts that man chooses to do evil "of necessity." This was the contradiction he set out to expose. On Jenyns's first letter, which invokes the principle of plenitude, Johnson does not waste words. He quickly sees that the existence of a God "infinitely powerful, wise and benevolent" is taken for granted even though this is what the enquiry is to demonstrate. Jenyns and Pope both claim that evil is part of a universal system and that good could not have been produced exclusive of evil, recalls Johnson, yet the claim is inadequate since to our limited comprehension they might have been mixed in various degrees, and "the degree of evil might have been less without any impediment to the good."[14]

With the second letter, he is more thorough as he introduces the reader to the scale of being, his principal target. If there are beings of every possible sort, Johnson argues, then the greatest number possible of every sort should exist, yet we are able to observe that this is not even true of mankind. Of three orders of being, we cannot prove that the first and third receive any advantages from the second, so why are intermediate orders useful? We do not even know that they exist. The implications of the theory, what Jenyns calls the compensations of poverty, the advantages of ignorance, and the fitness of educating the rich, interest Johnson even more. Here, he loses his detachment, and his language becomes fervid.[15] He knows from his own experience that there is more to poverty than "want of riches" and can verify that the speculations of someone as comfortably placed as Jenyns are not likely to add to our knowledge of the subject. Furthermore, no madman would reject an offer to restore his own reason if he could, and no pauper should be condemned to ignorance simply because his father is poor.

Johnson has more to say about poverty in his discussion of the third letter, where he questions Jenyns's optimistic assertion that evil is a necessary part of the total happiness of the universe. Subordination does not imply imperfection, he replies: "The weed as a weed is no less perfect than the oak as an oak."[16] Consequently, imperfection does not produce evil unless it implies the absence of some good, in which case it only causes suffering with the sufferer's knowledge of his privation. In response to the assertion that the world could not subsist without poverty and that God permitted labor to exist to preserve us from idleness, he is quick to show that God could just as easily have prevented poverty. "Where has this enquirer added to the little knowledge that we had before,'' thunders Johnson. "He has told us of the benefits of evil, which no man feels, and relations between distant parts of the universe, which he cannot himself conceive."[17] For Johnson, the purpose of a study of evil is either to enable the reader to enjoy life better or to endure it better, and Jenyns has not succeeded in doing either.

In the final instalment of his review, Johnson considers the last three letters. He is pleased with Jenyns's description of vice and virtue and takes pleasure in quoting it at length, but he cannot agree with his assertion that actions are to be judged in terms of their consequences as long as we cannot see what will ultimately produce happiness. As an orthodox Christian, Johnson declares that this is the purpose of revelation, to lay down a rule to be followed invariably "in opposition to appearances, and in every change of circumstances" so that we may be prevented from the mistake of doing evil in order to promote good. He finds nothing new in the letter on political evils and sees nothing more in the letter on religious evils than what Jenyns has learned from "the divines." He therefore concludes that while there may be some reason for the existence of evil, that reason has escaped our knowledge, the theory of the scale of being and its underlying principles being too speculative and too facile to help us understand such a complex problem. By doing so, he demonstrates the insufficiency of Jenyns's work on empirical grounds. While the *Free Inquiry* may have philosophical pretensions, he seems to say, it is not a work of faith, for Jenyns has appealed to experience and confounded his argument by basing it on a Platonic metaphysic.

An Apology for Christianity

The writing of "evidences" of Christianity began as a form of response to deism and continued until the third decade of the nineteenth century.[18] In these tracts, evidentialists responded to deist doubts about the historical authenticity of Christianity by claiming that the life of Christ was a form of divine revelation, particularly as it was shown forth in the miracles recorded in the New Testament, the most important of which was the Resurrection. They first set out to authenticate the Scriptures with reference to the witness of the early church; then they appealed to the content of the Scriptures as a medium of revelation. This historical criticism led to a closer study of the New Testament and a consideration of the apostolic age disclosed therein. In response to rationalist claims, it consequently constructed a rationale for Christian belief by drawing certain deductions from events reputed to have taken place. According to the common thesis manifested in such works, God had revealed his commandments and his intentions for mankind through a kind of cosmic sign language that included mighty works and wonderful events, the life of Christ itself being one such instrument.

Soame Jenyns's *View of the Internal Evidence of the Christian Religion* is a typical evidentialist "proof" of this sort and therefore a much more orthodox work than the *Free Inquiry*. Still, Jenyns ignored such evidences as prophecy and miracle, evidences usually encountered in similar works, and concentrated on what he called "internal evidence"—that which could be inferred from the nature of Christian ethics. Eighteenth-century humanist ethics, it should be remembered, still took into account the possibility of eternal life. The life hereafter was still viewed as a place for meting out rewards and punishments according to the requirements demanded by civil society and the qualities considered appropriate for an upright life. Jenyns's *View of the Internal Evidence* must be read in this context, and indeed it was its ethical emphasis that prompted Paley, probably the most influential evidentialist at the close of the eighteenth century, to announce that he would willingly transcribe its remarks on the morality of the gospel into his own work, *A View of the Evidences of Christianity* (1794), because "it perfectly agrees with my own opinion, and because it is impossible to say the same things so well."[19] Jenyns's rather utilitarian apologetic appealed to common sense in restating a familiar argument: without denying the truth of prophecy and miracle, it contended that the truth of the Christian religion could be demonstrated by showing the "internal marks of divinity" stamped on it, "because on this the credibility of the prophecies and miracles in a great measure depends." Jenyns, therefore, does not seek to undermine the credibility of prophecies and miracles. He allows that much of their credibility depends on "the truth of that religion, whose credibility they were at first intended to support" (4:5).

Jenyns's argumentative method is the analogical method employed with such force in Bishop Butler's *Analogy of Religion, Natural and Revealed, to the Constitution and Course of Nature* (1736), where Butler contended that both natural and revealed religion had laid open a scheme not unlike the one revealed by nature itself. In similar fashion, Jenyns argues that just as we see God's handiwork manifested in the heavens and the earth, we also see a scheme of religion and morality superior to anything that could be contrived by the human mind or discovered by human knowledge and must therefore conclude that it originated with the same omnipotent and omniscient being. Like Butler, he minimizes the power of scientific evidence to demonstrate anything absolutely, recalling how men often act from day to day without certain knowledge. And so, he applies the rule of probability not only to matters of practice but to matters of speculation. He assumes the existence of an intelligent creator *a priori*, but although he grants the existence of evidence derived from prophecy and miracle, he is primarily interested in what may be learned from a survey of human experience. This "internal evidence" leads him to a belief in God's existence as well as a belief in His moral purpose and the consequent duty of man.

Jenyns's analysis of what constitutes Christian ethics extends the discussion of virtue begun in the fourth letter of the *Free Inquiry*, one that had impressed Johnson so much that he reprinted ten pages of it in his review.[20] There, Jenyns argued that the *consequences* of men's actions determined their value and that while the end of virtue was to produce happiness, the ultimate end was the opportunity provided men by the creator to exalt or degrade themselves in this state as a probation for a rank of higher perfection or greater misery. The test of worthiness was doing good. This time, however, by laying so much emphasis on the rewards of virtuous behavior, Jenyns appears to ignore the other signs of revelation, prophecy and miracles, granting them only cursory attention. And Johnson, who had once applauded him on the subject, was not satisfied this time. "What Soame Jenyns says upon this subject is not to be minded;" he said, "he is a wit. No, Sir; to act from pure benevolence is not possible for finite beings. Human benevolence is mingled with vanity, interest, or some other motive."[21] In the place of traditional virtues like valor, patriotism, and friendship, Jenyns substitutes Christian virtues more apt to "prepare" us for the kingdom of heaven: poorness of spirit, forgiveness of injuries, charity to all men, repentance, faith, self-abasement, and detachment from the world. Such an ethical system as this, he proposes, could not have been invented by man. It is so foreign to what the human mind would conceive that it must have been created by a divine power.

Once again, Jenyns appeals to what is reasonable: not the reasonableness of a structured universe inferred from that part of the universe we see about us but the reasonableness that tells us man's capacities are limited. Why should the early Christians have attempted to propagate a religion of their own accord without divine inspiration? No reasonable person could believe they turned imposters to propagate truth, villains to teach honesty, and martyrs with no expectation of honor. Finally, the long commentary serving as a conclusion assumes the presence of a perfect God communicating a religion to an imperfect creature who is ill-equipped to understand the ways of his maker and unable to perceive the whole of creation. We must not depend upon our reason as an aid to faith, says Jenyns. We must acknowledge the practical benefits to be gained from the practice of religion: a preservation against vicious habits, a haven for those in distress, a basis for contemplation. To those who believe there is some truth in Christianity even though they cannot overcome their objections—"all those busy or idle persons, whose time and thoughts are wholly engrossed by the pursuits of business or pleasure, ambition or luxury" (4:114)—the book is meant to offer enlightenment and hope.

The long conclusion is a defense against certain deistic objections to Christianity: the needlessness of revelation, the fallibility of the Scriptures, the conflict between Christian ethics and the passions of mankind, the transformation of religion throughout the centuries, and the incredibility of certain articles of faith. In the first instance, Jenyns denies that reason is a sufficient guide to morality, pointing out that it makes no progress toward moral knowledge by itself. Morality is the special mark of civilization: other forms of human progress have followed where Christianity has spread while heathens endowed with reason have languished in a barbarous state. As for the errors and inconsistencies detected by critics of the Scriptures, he finds that they are not attributable to revelation but to the imperfections of man and therefore do not diminish the intrinsic excellence of the Bible. To the charge that Christianity is ill-suited to the passions and inclinations of mankind he replies by appealing to the doctrine of a future state, drawing on the familiar argument that Christianity is not a code of laws for a well-ordered society but primarily an institution to conduct us through the sufferings of sin and temptation and to prepare us for future happiness. Its end is not public utility but rather a means of accumulating merit against the time we are ready to be "transplanted" elsewhere. What of the alleged perversion and corruption of Christianity in its original state? The ignorance of the early Christians caused early adherents to temper the faith with their own superstitions and opinions, he explains, and the process could not have been altered without a series of miracles or an alteration in human nature. Still, Christianity has nevertheless diminished vice and corrected men's evil dispositions in spite of such ignorance and would eventually wipe out sin and punishment if it were adopted universally. Finally, there is a defense of divine authority against the charge that doctrines such as the Trinity and the Atonement are incredible. Once again, Jenyns appeals to the limitation of human comprehension and allows that propositions contradicting *our* reason may still be true. Though he distrusts reason alone as a guide to morality, he leaves no doubt about the role of reason in understanding doctrines of this kind. "Reason is undoubtedly our surest guide in all matters, which lie within the narrow circle of her intelligence:" he writes. "On the subject of revelation her province is only to examine into its authority; and when that is once proved, she has no more to do, but to acquiesce in its doctrines; and therefore is never so ill employed, as when she pretends to accommodate them to her own ideas of rectitude and truth" (4:111).

The *View of the Internal Evidence*, except for denying the value of certain virtues usually admired and bringing forward others usually condemned, is not an original work of religious thought but an ethical tract employing analogical reasoning and proceeding carefully along a *via media* between revelation and natural religion. It appeals to the reader's sense of the historical excellence of the early church and the virtuous behavior of Christians throughout the centuries in recommending that such virtue is to be practiced for the benefit of the world and for the sake of assuring man's happiness in a future state. While reason may not confirm this, it argues, one should nevertheless have faith and accept the limitations of both reason and perception in comprehending the workings of God. When he reached this same conclusion in the *Free Inquiry*, Jenyns advised the reader to submit and accept the inevitability of evil in the world while striving to reform moral behavior. This time, he advises him to have faith while adopting more genuine though more difficult Christian virtues so as to secure happiness in the afterlife.

Disquisitions on Several Subjects

Disquisitions on Several Subjects (1782) was a collection of short essays on Jenyns's favorite philosophical and political themes combined in a single volume. With one or two exceptions, they were restatements of familiar arguments appearing in his previous publications, and they did not reveal any alteration or development in his thought after his retirement from Parliament.[22] Following upon the widely read *View of the Internal Evidence*, the book alarmed certain readers when it appeared and provoked others to charge the author with sophistry and infidelity. The apparent lack of consistency perplexed those accustomed to regarding Jenyns as the champion of orthodoxy. As John Young wrote, "such disquisitions could not have been reasonably expected from *you*, without an explicit recantation of the only just, and therefore the only valuable part of your View of Christianity."[23] Young was undoubtedly referring to the choice of subjects discussed therein, including the chain of universal being, a preexistent state, and the analogy between things material and intellectual, subjects that seemed to recapture the rationalistic flavor of the *Free Inquiry*. In presenting these to the public, some of them for the second time, Jenyns seemed to imply that his tract on the Christian religion was an anomaly.

As the first disquisition shows, although Jenyns had not attempted a direct answer to Johnson's analysis of the chain of being, that did not mean he had abandoned it. In this essay on the "chain of universal being," he portrays the Creator as an infinitely wise and powerful "divine artificer" and carefully defines the system of subordination He is supposed to have created, using the language adopted for the *Free Inquiry*. Yet he draws no ethical or political conclusions. Instead, he details the orders of earthly creatures (matter, vegetation, animals, and man) rising above each other by degrees and places man at the top, superior by virtue of his reason yet sharing the qualities of his inferiors. He then confines his discussion to only one of the supporting principles of the theory, continuity, and proceeds to emphasize one other feature, the position of man at the midpoint of the scale as a whole. From there he imagines "through the perspective of analogy and conjecture" that other beings exist in the grades above him. How man makes contact with these beings he never explains, but we are nevertheless assured that they are there, ranging in their variety from inhabitants of other planets to angels and archangels, their lowest orders united with the highest of ours and their reason amply supplemented with intuitive knowledge and other "faculties" we cannot imagine. These two claims—that man possesses some qualities of inferior animals and that he acts as a "link" between spiritual and corporeal beings—leads appropriately to the next section, devoted to the subject of cruelty to "inferior" animals.

The Pythagorean theory of a link between man and beast was a belief not uncommonly held during the eighteenth century, and it owed its popularity chiefly to the spread of Montaigne's essays.[24] The theory seems to have appealed to Jenyns from an early date. In the "Epistle to Lord Lovelace," he had denounced at length the roistering of his rural neighbors as dull and offensive, singling out hunting and cockfighting as particularly despicable practices. In *World* no. 163, an essay on the transmigration of souls, he had taken great pleasure in imagining sportsmen who had entertained themselves with the miseries of "innocent" animals suddenly shaking with terror in some future state when metamorphosed into hares, partridges, and woodcocks. There he had heaped invective upon the heads of such sportsmen for their wanton destructiveness and ingratitude and, in a particularly sentimental passage, had cited some common instances of abuse. "The social and friendly dog is hanged without remorse," he wrote, "if, by barking in defense of his master's person and property, he happens unknowingly to disturb his rest; the generous horse, who has carried his ungrateful master for many years with ease and safety, worn out with age and infirmities contracted in his service, is by him condemned to end his miserable days in a dustcart, where the more he exerts his little remains of spirit, the more he is whipped, to save his stupid driver the trouble of whipping some other, less obedient to the lash" (3:188). In the present essay, he argues that animals should be destroyed only in self-defense, and when they must be killed for man's survival, they should be dispatched with tenderness and compassion. He attributes man's disposition to kill to his "fallen" state, which he brings with him into the world, and notes that we may observe it more easily in those living a life approximating a "state of nature"—children, savages, and common people. For sheer feeling, none of Jenyns's prose equals this short piece. Only one other subject could draw forth such feeling, and that was the subject of the next section on a "preexistent" state.

The belief in a preexistent state, for which Jenyns constructs a respectable pedigree here, is basic to Jenyns's thought, and it recurs from time to time throughout his works. It receives its most graphic treatment in *World* no. 163, where Jenyns declares it has always been "a favourite of mine" and "one of the most rational guesses" about the nature of a future state. The theory of the transmigration of souls assumes a preexistent state, and Jenyns justifies such a state for its justice and utility and for providing an opportunity to redress the sufferings of innocent creatures. But how is such a theory to be reconciled with reason, with what we see around us, and with revelation? Working on the premise that an immortal soul existing after the dissolution of the body must have existed eternally before the creation of the body, he falls back upon a Platonic argument he has used before. Since infinite power cannot be employed without a design, he says, the world as we know it (whose design we may observe) must have been designed as a "prison" to punish us for offenses committed in a preexistent state and to allow us the chance to prepare ourselves for a future one. Natural disasters in the world and the wretchedness of human life confirm for him the likelihood that we are "committed" here for varying periods of time and for labors of varying severity. In what has become by now a characteristic imaginative leap, he looks around him and sums up the whole history of mankind as little more than the aggregate of its miseries, and as he details the awful catalog of plague, famine, flood, earthquake, war, and malevolence of all kinds, he likens the victims to "condemned criminals" in receipt of their punishment, sometimes meted out at each other's hands. The bizarre image of exiled spirits confined in this world eventually becomes reconciled to the teachings of Christianity when it is linked to the depravity of man and the redemptive act of Christ. It also provides a further explanation for the existence of evil. Jenyns could now conclude that the world is evil because it has been designed as a place of punishment.

Disquisition IV, on the nature of time, and Disquisition V, on the analogy between material and intellectual things, are further exercises in Jenyns's analogical method. In the first instance, Jenyns defines time as a "mode" of existence, a "delusion" of the imagination. He suggests that there are two modes of existence: the one in which we find ourselves and another he calls "Eternity," one that may be inhabited by "superior orders of created beings." This distinction allows him to clear up certain theological and metaphysical mysteries, including predestination, preexistent and future states, the injustice of eternal punishments, and the sleep of the soul. It is particularly useful for supporting his notion that there are beings on faraway planets and beneath the ocean whose existence is incomprehensible to us, for he then may suppose "time may be no more necessary to existence than water, though the mode of that existence we are unable to comprehend" (3:231). In the next disquisition, he again employs the analogical method to support the proposition that there are "powers and propensities of a similar nature" operating throughout upon things material, moral, and political. After an elaborate series of examples purporting to show how balance is achieved both in nature and in the lives of men, Jenyns reveals how they show forth the remarkable "oeconomy of things," the "art" of its omnipotent creator.

The sixth disquisition, written on the subject of rational Christianity, is indeed a curious outburst, not against deists but against rationalist theologians. Without knowing what provoked it, the reader might almost take it as a defense of Jenyns's own methodology. In effect, it attempts to refute Christian apologists bent on reconciling reason with revelation. By striving to reduce revelationary doctrines to human understanding, he charges, rationalist theologians have succeeded only in reducing Christianity to deism, revelation being a form of information not adaptable to reason. He therefore adopts the Pauline attitude that the religion of the New Testament is a "mystery." Rationalist theologians, he finds, have substituted for revealed Christianity a system of ethics so as to court acceptance and by so doing have assassinated it "in the dark."

The final item of this collection (the seventh is discussed in chapter 5), though an essay on religious establishments, should be seen within the context of Jenyns's political ideas. From a conservative viewpoint, it directs itself toward the advocates of increased religious liberty who were promoting the expansion of liberties granted Dissenters by the Act of Toleration. Aware that such demands constituted one of the changes recommended by parliamentary reformers in his own constituency, Jenyns regarded them suspiciously as radical gestures threatening the stability of government rather than as genuine religious concerns. While conceding that the individual is accountable to God alone in matters of conviction and conscience and that government has no right to control such matters, he nevertheless allows that government must take notice of them "whenever they shoot up into actions" since religious principles related to power and liberty are "common combustibles" used to inflame the foolish and the ignorant when religion is not at issue. By establishing one set of doctrines to be part of a constitution with unlimited toleration of others, he writes, government cools these contentions, not because religion and government enjoy a natural connection but because establishment will prevent other alliances based on ignorance and superstition. Similarly, he finds that Christianity is a suitable religion on which a nation should fix its establishment because it bears the sanctions of supernatural authority and shows a marked superiority to other "fabulous" systems.

These disquisitions, though ostensibly addressed to a variety of philosophical questions, are really elaborations of one or two ideas that Jenyns continued to hold in later life. Throughout them we encounter the now familiar structure of the great chain of being, the image of life as a middle state designed to punish preexistent wrongs and to enable the wrongdoer to qualify for a future state, the process of the transmigration of souls, and the affirmation that we can know these things by analogical reasoning even though we are handicapped by our limited perception and knowledge. Nevertheless, Jenyns is still unwilling to consider himself a promoter of "rational Christianity" even though his language and his ideas would lead the reader to think that he is.

Chapter Seven
Conclusion

By the last decade of the eighteenth century, Soame Jenyns had come to be regarded as a competent if limited satiric poet and a prose stylist of some accomplishment. Selected poems could still be read in anthologies compiled by such editors as Robert Dodsley, Mark Akenside, and Sir Charles Hanbury Williams; a four-volume edition of his complete works could be had; and a place had been secured for him in the great collections of the British poets that had begun to appear. The week he died, the *Morning Chronicle* had attributed to Burke the opinion that Jenyns was one of those who wrote the "purest" English, a style of writing unaffected by foreign influence. There were those who ranked him with Beattie, Blair, and Chesterfield as a practitioner of the graceful, mandarin style. Yet this reputation rested almost exclusively on Jenyns's ability to be witty and amusing, no matter how grave the subject under discussion. Whether in conversation or in print, he seemed to prefer the paradoxical and the ironic and to dwell upon the ridiculous. Indeed, his long career in Parliament presented him with numerous opportunities to do so, and he succeeded in making a name for himself among his fellow members as something of a court jester rather than a man of influence and leadership. At all times, he was a self-conscious gentleman cultivating the gentlemanly qualities of elegance and restraint, not only in his public duties but in his private life, and he showed forth his gentlemanly point of view in his publications. Gradually, his verses settled into the category reserved for "curious" and "fugitive" pieces and for "wit"; his essays and pamphlets lost touch with contemporary thought. As his life's work as a writer was duly recorded and

Conclusion

annotated, his editor warmly predicted, "As an author, so long as a true taste of fine writing shall exist, he will have a distinguished place amongst those who have excelled." By the turn of the century, however, his reputation was already beginning to fade. Why was this so?

To begin with, Jenyns confined himself almost exclusively to an ironic tone typical of early eighteenth-century authors, his intentions being almost always satiric, and he maintained this ironic attitude with subtlety and refinement. He appeared before the reader as an ideal gentleman adopting the conversational style of a cultivated man of taste, rendering his jesting and raillery more likely to please than to offend. Even when he censured, he maintained an air of ease and negligence. Except for the poems circulated privately, he attacked human failings so general or imaginary and aberrations so minor that no individual could take exception. He thus seemed to be acting out of a spirit of friendly affection or good-natured interest and a desire to entertain.

We first encounter his playfulness in his early poetry. From the light verse of his early years, best exemplified by the "Art of Dancing," Jenyns continued to work within such ironic forms as the mock-heroic poem, the burlesque imitation, the classical translation, and the "progress" piece while at the same time demonstrating a skill for parodying both classical and contemporary poets and an eye for the ridiculous in political and social behavior. Though these brief studies in political and social manners showed promise, Jenyns restrained himself from developing into a more incisive and far-reaching satirist. His gentlemanly style prevented him from doing so. His more stinging productions, such as his "Simile," his burlesque ode, and his epitaph on Dr. Johnson, suggested that something bolder was lurking within; but these were private displays contrived for the benefit of his friends, and their publication only served to confirm the impression that behind the polite public facade there was an imagination not fully exercised in the practice of social criticism.

When Jenyns therefore turned his attention more exclusively to prose upon entering the House of Commons, he had already fixed for himself something of a voice, making it difficult for his readers to know whether or not to take him seriously, for his prose featured the same blend of irony, facetiousness, and gentle mockery. Whether discussing parliamentary reform or the high cost of provisions, whether proclaiming the reality of a preexistent state or defending the imposition of the Stamp Act, he could be counted on to be entertaining and disarming. Jenyns further confused his readers by sitting for the Whig interest while at the same time espousing a set of principles not fully in keeping with the liberal Whig philosophy of the late seventeenth century. His more conservative view of society and government advocated the maintenance of the traditional landed gentry and its authority, the continuance of a form of royal prerogative, and the preservation of a parliamentary system unaffected by the reform movement alive in the country. He preferred to regard politics as an art to be practiced with skill, delicacy, compromise, and influence rather than a science controlled by a set of abstract principles, and he approached with some relish his dispute with Locke's second treatise of government. Uninfluenced by liberal political thought, he remained committed to a static, hierarchical social system that seemed to make no provision for alleviating the common ills of daily life. Instead, by taking eighteenth-century optimism to its extreme, he seemed to be arguing that the ills experienced by ordinary people might somehow be good.

Jenyns espoused custom and practice in public affairs at the expense of fostering change. His political philosophy was grounded in the observation and experience of parliamentary politics, and as a result he appealed to the stability of public institutions rather than the urges of nature (which he judged to be faulty and base) as a means of continuing a civilized society. In denying the principle of social contract, he denied the liberal logic that would justify challenge to authority merely on the basis of an abstract theory assuming men to exist equally in a state of nature. Governments were delicate instruments contrived for protecting the very benefits for which men banded together in societies, he contended; they were not the changeable handmaidens of human needs but the constant protectors of those needs.

And since they had developed gradually over a period of time, they had acquired the advantages that could come only with experience. Violent change was anathema to them. Thus, Jenyns's distaste for antagonism and party strife permitted him to countenance the notion of "party" only as a necessity. Instead, he readily accepted the system of "influence" that activated British politics during the period of Whig supremacy, a system of patronage and pensions, corruption and bribes, family connections and prerogative that had somehow promoted a state of equilibrium beneath the turbulent surface of parliamentary life. In his political thought, he therefore applauded the useful and the efficacious.

When Jenyns turned his attention to metaphysics, he found that his reputation as a wit had become something of a handicap. In his early career, he was clearly moved by the rationalism of the times: both the "Essay on Virtue" and the *Free Inquiry* bore the imprint of natural religion. The *Free Inquiry* in particular, ostensibly a discourse on ethics, assumed the existence of a divine artificer and a universe manifesting his design. When, at length, the *View of the Internal Evidence* subsequently appeared as a tract defending orthodox Christianity, critics were at a loss to know whether to take it seriously or not. It did receive an approving word from the sovereign before taking hold as a fashionable book in the upper reaches of society, and it did enjoy considerable attention as a topic of discussion, prolonged for more than a year by the controversy played out by commentators in the magazines and newspapers. Moreover, it did arrive on the scene at a time when the orthodox were ready to welcome a book that seemed to counter some of the claims of natural religion, for it gave assurances that the religion of the New Testament was grounded in the divine. However, the *View of the Internal Evidence* still confused discerning and knowledgeable readers, not least because Jenyns had not managed to separate himself convincingly from his public image as a trivializer, ridiculer, and parodist. Was he serious this time or not? One could not be sure. And the confusion was compounded a few years later with the publication of *Disquisitions on Several Subjects*, for now he seemed ready to return to his former preoccupations. *Disquisitions* was not only couched in paradoxical and ironic language but founded on speculative metaphysical notions. It concluded with an attack on rationalist theologians, themselves engaged in the struggle against the claims of natural theology.

Soame Jenyns's most prominent feature as a writer is his wit. His poems are light and amusing and his prose correct and refined; nevertheless, this quality has not been sufficient to sustain him over the years. When, at the end of the eighteenth century, a radical change in taste occurred and the literature of the preceding age suffered the disparagement of Romantic critics, Jenyns's verse lay neglected. His pamphlets had lost their currency, and his philosophical works no longer seemed applicable to the spirit of the times. Only the *View of the Internal Evidence* continued to be read in the early nineteenth century as a textbook for undergraduates and an inspirational tract for evangelicals. Today, a poem such as "The Modern Fine Gentleman" enjoys a revival from time to time in anthologies of satire; but otherwise, the poet himself commands no special attention except as the victim of Johnson's review or the source of the infamous "epitaph." Yet he does reflect for us in many ways the conservative preoccupations of his era as a promoter of reasoned belief over unbelief, stability over violent change, and, above all, virtue and polite manners over antagonism and strife.

Notes and References

Chapter One

1. See Samuel Wells, *The History of the Drainage of the Great Level of the Fens, Called Bedford Level* (London: R. Pheney, 1830), and H. C. Darby, *The Draining of the Fens* (Cambridge: Cambridge University Press, 1940).
2. Cambridgeshire Record Office, R.59.31.9.1, minutes of adventurers' proceedings, and R.59.31.6.A, letter books signed by Roger Jenyns and petition dated 1 July 1669. See also C.R.O., Q/RDz 5, f. 210 ff. and 267 ff., enclosure awards, and Q/RDc 12, enclosure map. A sometimes inaccurate history of the Jenyns family appears in Edward Hailstone's *History . . . of the Parish of Bottisham* (Cambridge, 1873), pp. 118–29, with a genealogical table. A precise description of the estate with photographs appears in *An Inventory of Historical Monuments in the County of Cambridge* (London: HMSO, 1972), 2:6–8.
3. British Library Add. MS. 5805, f. 20.
4. C. N. Cole, "Sketches of the Life of Soame Jenyns, Esq.," in Jenyns, *Works* (London, 1790), 1:xvii, hereafter cited as "Sketches."
5. "Collections for an Athenae Cantabrigienses," B.L. Add. MS. 5873, f. 55.
6. Jenyns family papers, Bottisham Hall.
7. Cole, "Sketches," p. xx, but cf. B.L. Add. MS. 5883, f. 164, where the Reverend William Cole claims the second tutor was the latter's illustrious brother, the Reverend John White, who died in 1755.
8. John E. B. Mayor and Robert F. Scott, eds., *Admissions to the College of St. John the Evangelist in the University of Cambridge* (Cambridge: Cambridge University Press, 1882–1931), 3:34.
9. See D. A. Winstanley, *Unreformed Cambridge: A Study of Certain Aspects of the University in the Eighteenth Century* (Cambridge: Cambridge University Press, 1935), especially pp. 198–99.

10. John Venn and J. A. Venn, eds., *Alumni Cantabrigienses* (Cambridge: Cambridge University Press, 1922–54), pt. 1, 2:471.

11. Soame Jenyns, *Works* (London, 1790), 2:136; subsequent references are to this edition.

12. B.L. Add. MS. 5843, f. 94.

13. B.L. Loan MS. 29/326. Lady Margaret was the daughter of the earl of Oxford.

14. One song had already been published in *A Collection of Original Scotch Songs, with a Thorough Bass to each Song, for the Harpsichord* (London, 1726?), a variation of his "Snowball. From Petronius Afranius."

15. B.L. Add. MS. 5873, f. 55.

16. See Francis Blomefield, *An Essay Towards a Topographical History of the County of Norfolk* (Fersfield, Norwich, and Lynn, 1739–75), 4:86–87, and "Extracts from a MS. Diary of Peter Le Neve, Esq.," *Norfolk Archaeology* 2 (1849):111, n. 1.

17. C.R.O., P18/1/4, Burwell parish register.

18. B.L. Add. MS. 5873, f. 55, and Romney Sedgwick, *The House of Commons, 1715–1754* (London: HMSO, 1970), 2:213–14.

19. *Gentleman's Magazine* 20 (1750):283.

20. Ibid., 23 (1753): 392, and *Cambridge Journal*, 4 August 1753.

21. B.L. Add. MS. 5873, f. 55.

22. See L. B. Namier, *England in the Age of the American Revolution*, 2d ed. (London: Macmillan, 1961), pp. 18–26.

23. Daniel Cook, "The Representative History of the County, Town and University of Cambridge, 1689–1832" (Ph.D. diss., London University, 1935), p. 4.

24. Ibid., p. 21.

25. B.L. Add. MS. 5873, f. 55.

26. B.L. Add. MS. 35397, f. 58: Philip Yorke to Thomas Birch, 19 July 1747.

27. Horace Walpole, *The Yale Edition of Horace Walpole's Correspondence*, ed. W. S. Lewis (New Haven: Yale University Press, 1937–83), 30:312, 318.

28. Thomas Gray, *Correspondence*, ed. Paget Toynbee and Leonard Whibley (Oxford: Clarendon Press, 1935), 1:298.

29. *Monthly Review* 2 (1749–50):112.

30. Gray, *Correspondence*, 1:344; Hester L. Thrale, *Thraliana. The Diary of Mrs. Hester Lynch Thrale (Later Mrs. Piozzi) 1776–1809*, ed. Katherine C. Balderston (Oxford: Clarendon Press, 1942), 2:1053.

31. *Monthly Review* 6 (1752):211.
32. Sir Egerton Brydges, *Restituta; or, Titles, Extracts, and Characters of Old Books in English Literature, Revived* (London: Longman, Hurst, Rees, Orme & Brown, 1814–16), 3:38.
33. Cook, "Representative History," passim.
34. B.L. Add. MS. 35351, f. 228: Hardwicke to Philip Yorke, 30 June 1753.
35. B.L. Add. MS. 35679, f. 268: Downing to Hardwicke, 25 June 1758.
36. James Boswell, *The Life of Samuel Johnson, LL.D.*, ed. Edmond Malone (London: Jones & Co., 1829), p. 56, n.
37. Richard Cumberland, *Memoirs* (London: Printed for Lackington, Allen & Co., 1806), pp. 247–48.
38. [Elizabeth Sheridan], *Betsy Sheridan's Journal: Letters from Sheridan's sister 1784–1786 and 1788–1790*, ed. William Lefanu (London: Eyre & Spottiswoode, 1960), p. 43.
39. B.L. Add. MS. 5873, f. 56, and Walpole, *Correspondence*, 2:58. This portrait now hangs in Bottisham Hall.
40. B.L. Add. MS. 5873, f. 55.
41. Cumberland, *Memoirs*, pp. 248–49. Gibbon was also fond of this anecdote. See Edward Gibbon, *Letters*, ed. J. E. Norton (London: Cassell, 1956), 2:396.
42. William Roberts, *Memoirs of the Life and Correspondence of Mrs. Hannah More*, 2d ed. (London: R. B. Seeley & W. Burnside, 1834), 4:242–43.
43. Sir James Prior, *Life of Edmond Malone, Editor of Shakespeare* (London: Smith, Elder & Co., 1860), pp. 375–76.
44. John Russell, duke of Bedford, *Correspondence* (London: Longman et al., 1842–46), 3:220: Rigby to Bedford, 10 March 1763.
45. Benjamin Franklin, *Private Correspondence* (London: Henry Colburn, 1817), 1:293: to William Franklin, 28 August 1767.
46. Walpole, *Correspondence*, 30:47.
47. "Joseph Farington's Anecdotes of Walpole 1793–1797," in Walpole, *Correspondence*, 15:331.
48. Walpole, *Correspondence*, 28:82, 86.
49. James Boswell, *Boswell's Life of Johnson*, ed. G. B. Hill, rev. L. F. Powell (Oxford: Clarendon Press, 1934–50; 1964), 1:315.
50. Hester L. Piozzi, *Autobiography, Letters and Literary Remains of Mrs. Piozzi (Thrale)*, ed. A. Hayward (London: Longman et al., 1861), 1:121, 122.
51. *The Monitor, or British Freeholder*, no. 187, 17 February

1759, pp. 1128 f. Cf. Swift's *Intelligencer*, no. 188, p. 1138.

52. B.L. Add. MS. 35399, f. 169: Birch to Royston, 4 October 1760.

53. Horace Walpole, *Memoirs of the Reign of King George the Second*, ed. Lord Holland (London: Henry Colburn, 1847), 3:179.

54. Walpole, *Correspondence*, 29:32-33, 50, 100, 155.

55. James Boswell, *The Yale Editions of the Private Papers of James Boswell*, ed. Marshall Waingrow (London: Heinemann, 1969), 2:252.

56. Mrs. Mary Delany, *Autobiography and Correspondence*, ed. Lady Llanover (London: Richard Bentley, 1861-62), 6:348. See also Cumberland, *Memoirs*, pp. 248-49. There is evidence that the last word is a euphemism. See Mahmoud Manzalaoui, "Soame Jenyns's 'Epitaph on Dr. Samuel Johnson,'" *Notes and Queries* 212 (1967):181-82.

57. See *Gentleman's Magazine* 56 (1786):428, and Boswell, *Boswell's Life of Johnson*, 1:316, n. 2.

58. *Gentleman's Magazine* 56 (1786):696, and John Courtenay, *A Poetical Review of the Literary and Moral Character of the Late Samuel Johnson, L.L.D.* (London, 1786), p. 15.

Chapter Two

1. Mary P. Clarke, "The Board of Trade at Work," *American Historical Review* 17 (1911):20-21.

2. A. H. Basye, *The Lords Commissioners of Trade and Plantations* (New Haven: Yale University Press, 1925), pp. 220-29.

3. Walpole, *Memoirs of the Reign of King George the Second*, 2:140.

4. B.L. Add. MS. 35631, f. 7: Jenyns to Hardwicke, 27 July 1756.

5. See C. M. Andrews, *The Colonial Period of American History* (New Haven: Yale University Press, 1964), vol. 4, chap. 9.

6. Cumberland, *Memoirs*, p. 186, and Edward Gibbon, *Memoirs of My Life*, ed. Georges A. Bonnard (London: Nelson, 1966), p. 161.

7. *Cobbett's Parliamentary History of England* (London: R. Bagshaw et al., 1806-20), 21:238.

8. Gibbon, *Memoirs*, p. 173.

9. Prior, *Life of Edmond Malone*, p. 375.

10. *Monthly Review* 16 (1757):304; "Philagathos," *Necessity*,

not the origin of evil, religious or moral (London, 1757), pp. 3-4, 36; Gray, *Correspondence*, 2:499: to William Mason, 23 April 1757; [Richard Shepherd], *The Review of a Free Enquiry into the Nature and Origin of Evil* (London, 1759), p. 10; *A Letter to the Author of a Free Enquiry into the Nature and Origin of Evil* (London, [1759]), p. 1.

11. Boswell, *Boswell's Life of Johnson*, 1:315.
12. *Literary Magazine* 2 (1757):302.
13. See Donald J. Greene, "Johnson's Contributions to the *Literary Magazine*," *Review of English Studies* 7 (1956):367-92.
14. Boswell, *Boswell's Life of Johnson*, 1:315.
15. John Nichols, *Literary Anecdotes of the Eighteenth Century* (London: Nichols, 1812-15), 4:647, n.; *Critical Review* 3 (1757):448.
16. David Hume, *Letters*, ed. J. Y. T. Greig (Oxford: Clarendon Press, 1932), 1:303, 312.
17. *Gentle Reflections upon the Short but Serious Reasons for a National Militia* (London, 1757), pp. 1-2.
18. B.L. Add. MS. 32882, f. 430: Kinnoul to Newcastle, 18 August 1758.
19. See also [William Bollan], *The Mutual Interest of Great Britain and the American Colonies Considered* (London, 1765).
20. [Daniel Dulany], *Considerations on the Propriety of Imposing Taxes in the British Colonies* (Annapolis, 1765), pp. 6 ff.
21. F. A., *Considerations on Behalf of the Colonists* (London, 1765), p. 9.
22. See Allen T. Hazen, *A Catalogue of Horace Walpole's Library* (London: Oxford University Press, 1969), 2:11. Written in Walpole's copy is the note "By Dr. Fothergill."
23. [John Fothergill?], *Reflexions on Representation in Parliament* (London, 1766), p. 13.
24. Sir John Fortescue, ed., *The Correspondence of King George the Third From 1760 to December 1783* (London: Macmillan, 1927-28), 1:93, 154.
25. J. R. G. Tomlinson, ed., *Additional Grenville Papers, 1763-65* (Manchester: Manchester University Press, 1962), p. 312: Grenville to Bamber Gascoyne, 12 July 1765.
26. B.L. Add. MS. 5873, f. 55.
27. [Reverend Samuel Peck?], *An Answer to a Pamphlet Intitled, "Thoughts on the Causes and Consequences of the present high Price of Provisions"* (London, 1768), pp. 27-28.
28. [George Lowe], *Considerations on the Effects which the Bounties Granted on Exported Corn, Malt, and Flour, have on*

the Manufactures of the Kingdom, and the True Interests of the State (London, 1768), pp. 75, 84, 96.

29. Cook, "Representative History," pp. 141–42.

30. Josiah Tucker, *An Humble Address and Earnest Appeal . . . Whether a Connection With, or a Separation from the Continental Colonies of America, Be Most for the National Advantage, and the Lasting Benefit of These Kingdoms* (Gloucester, 1775), p. 24. In 1783, there appeared an engraving depicting Fox's political conversion. It pictured him casting aside volumes of Locke and Sydney, indicating the overthrow of his constitutional and radical principles, and studying those of Jenyns and Tucker, works typifying supporters of the royal prerogative. See Mary Dorothy George, *Catalogue of Political and Personal Satires* (London: Trustees of the British Museum, 1935–54), 5:693–94.

31. B.L. Add. MS. 35631, f. 141: Jenyns to Hardwicke, 19 August 1775.

32. Delany, *Autobiography*, 5:184–85: Mrs. Boscawen to Mrs. Delany, 6 December 1775.

33. *Monthly Review* 70 (1784):378, and *European Magazine* 6 (1784):215.

34. *An Answer to Thoughts on a Parliamentary Reform* (London, 1784), p. 2.

35. *Some Other Thoughts on a Parliamentary Reform* (London, 1784), pp. 13, 14.

36. John Cartwright, *Internal Evidence; Or an Inquiry How Far Truth and the Christian Religion Have Been Consulted by the Author of Thoughts on a Parliamentary Reform* (London, 1784), pp. vii, 13.

37. See B.L. Add. MS. 35631, passim, and "An Original Journal of Mr Soame Jenyns" covering the years 1754 to 1786, preserved at Bottisham Hall.

38. B.L. Add. MS. 35631, f. 82: Jenyns to Hardwicke, 4 November 1769; f. 106: Jenyns to Hardwicke, 5 November 1771.

39. B.L. Add. MS. 5842, f. 116.

40. See B.L. Add. MS. 35631, f. 138: Jenyns to Hardwicke, 11 September 1774, and *Cambridge Chronicle and Journal*, 24 September 1774.

41. Walpole, *Correspondence*, 1:346: Cole to Walpole, 5 October 1774.

42. B.L. Add. MS. 5842, ff. 116–19, and *Cambridge Chronicle and Journal*, 15 October 1774.

43. B.L. Add. MS. 5842, f. 118.

44. B.L. Add. MS. 35631, f. 148: Jenyns to Hardwicke, 11 October 1774.

Chapter Three

1. James Boswell, *Private Papers of James Boswell from Malahide Castle*, ed. Geoffrey Scott and F. A. Pottle [New York: W. E. Rudge, 1928–34], 12:230.
2. John Nichols, *Literary Anecdotes*, 2:452, n.
3. Hyde Collection, Four Oaks Farm, Somerville, N.J. Copyright signed by Jenyns, 4 June 1776.
4. M. C. Tyler, *Patrick Henry* (Boston: Houghton, Mifflin, 1887), pp. 350–51.
5. Cole, "Sketches," pp. liv-lv.
6. Thrale, *Thraliana*, 1:96.
7. Peter O. Hutchinson, ed., *The Diary and Letters of His Excellency Thomas Hutchinson, Esq.* (London: Sampson Low, Marston, Searle & Rivington, 1883–86), 2:43.
8. Thomas Scott, *Works*, ed. John Scott (London: L. B. Seeley, 1823–25), 1:40; Boswell, *Private Papers*, 12:36.
9. James Beattie, *Letters* (London: John Sharpe, 1820), 2:25–26.
10. [Reverend William Jones of Nayland], *Observations in A Journey to Paris by Way of Flanders, In the Month of August 1776* (London, 1777), 1:188.
11. Walpole, *Correspondence*, 28:269.
12. Spencer Papers, Althorp: Mrs. Elizabeth Carter to Lady Georgiana Spencer, 29 July 1776; Prior, *Life of Edmond Malone*, p. 375.
13. Boswell, *Boswell's Life of Johnson*, 3:279–80, 288–90.
14. John Wesley, *Works* (London: Wesleyan Conference Office, 1872), 6:214, 4:82.
15. *Gentleman's Magazine* 46 (1776):273–75; *Monthly Review* 54 (1776):472; *Critical Review* 41 (1776):475.
16. *A Letter to Soame Jenyns, Esq.* (London, 1776), pp. 1, 29–30.
17. G. U., *A Letter to Soame Jenyns, Esq;* (London, 1776).
18. *An Essay on Valour* (London, 1776) and *Short Strictures on Certain Passages in A View of the Internal Evidence of the Christian Religion, By Soame Jenyns, Esq.* (London, 1776), p. 26.
19. *London Review of English and Foreign Literature* 3 (1776):508–28; Bodleian Library Add. MS. C. 90, ff. 40–41: Badcock to Ralph Griffiths, August 1780; and *Philosophical Disquisitions on the Christian Religion Addressed to Soame Jenyns, Esq. and W. Kenrick, L.L.D.* (London, 1777).
20. J. Mainwaring, *Sermons on Several Occasions, Preached Before the University of Cambridge* (Cambridge, 1780), p. lxxxv.

21. Archibald Maclaine, *A Series of Letters, Addressed to Soame Jenyns, Esq*; (London, 1777), pp. 4, 7–8.

22. Edward Fleet, *An Examination of the Arguments Contained in Dr. Maclaine's Answer to Soame Jenyns, Esq.* (London, 1777), p. 56.

23. Bodleian Library Add. MS. C. 89, f. 231: Maclaine to Griffiths, October 1777.

24. Percival Stockdale, *Six Discourses* (London, 1777), pp. 24–26. See also *Memoirs* (London: Longman et al., 1809), 2:106–8.

25. [Henry Taylor], *A Full Answer to a Late View of the Internal Evidence of the Christian Religion* (London, 1777), p. 2.

26. *Monthly Review* 67 (1782):81; *Critical Review* 53 (1782):364, 249.

27. *Gentleman's Magazine* 52 (1782):188; Walpole, *Correspondence* 29:198–99: to Mason, 14 March 1782; Roberts, *Memoirs*, 2:308; [Caesar Morgan], *Thoughts on a Pre-existent State, in Answer to a Late Disquisition on That Subject* (Cambridge, 1782), pp. 2–3.

28. Richard Watson, *Anecdotes of the Life of Richard Watson*, 2d ed. (London: T. Cadell & W. Davis, 1818), 1:143, and [Richard Watson], *An Answer to the Disquisition on Government and Civil Liberty* (London, 1782), p. 49.

29. *Monthly Review* 67 (1782):204.

30. Baptist Noel Turner, *Candid Suggestions; in Eight Letters to Soame Jenyns, Esq*; (London, 1782), p. 19.

31. John Nichols, *Illustrations of the Literary History of the Eighteenth Century* (London: Nichols, 1817–58), 6:167: Turner to Nichols, 15 November 1819.

32. Walpole, *Correspondence*, 29:200, 211.

33. "Malcolm MacGreggor," *An Archaeological Epistle to the Reverend and Worshipful Jeremiah Milles* (London, 1782), p. 14.

34. Gray, *Correspondence*, 2:546–47: Mason to Gray, 5 January 1758; Yale University Library, Benjamin Franklin Collection: Jenyns to Mason, 18 December [1762?].

35. Walpole, *Correspondence*, 29:241.

36. "Malcolm MacGreggor," *The Dean and the 'Squire: a Political Eclogue. Humbly Dedicated to Soame Jenyns, Esq.* (London, 1782), p. iv.

37. Walpole, *Correspondence*, 29:243–44: Walpole to Mason, 7 May 1782. Mason's manuscript is preserved in John Mitford's notebooks, B.L. Add. MS. 32563, ff. 83–94.

38. Ronald Rompkey, "Soame Jenyns, M.P.: A Curious Case of Membership," *Journal of the Royal Society of Arts* 120 (1972):536–42.

Notes and References

39. Henry R. Vassall, Lord Holland, *Further Memoirs of the Whig Party 1807–1821* (London: John Murray, 1905), p. 308.
40. Hannah More, *Works* (London: T. Cadell & W. Davies, 1801), 1:23.
41. Walpole, *Correspondence*, 29:104: Walpole to Mason, 5 February 1781; Lady Louisa Stuart, *Gleanings from an Old Portfolio*, ed. Mrs. Godfrey Clarke (Edinburgh: Privately Printed for David Douglas, 1895–98), 3:64.
42. Cumberland, *Memoirs*, p. 247.
43. Roberts, *Memoirs*, 1:76.
44. Frances Burney (Madame d'Arblay), *Memoirs of Doctor Burney* (London: Edward Moxon, 1832), 2:268.
45. Walpole, *Correspondence*, 29:287: Mason to Walpole, 5 March 1783; Roberts, *Memoirs*, 1:395: Hannah More to her sister, 1785.
46. Frances Burney, *Diary and Letters* (London: Henry Colburn, 1842–46), 2:242 f., and *Memoirs of Doctor Burney*, 2:289–90: to Samuel Crisp.
47. Burney, *Diary and Letters*, 2:247.
48. B.L. Add. MS. 35631, f. 207. The verse is printed in *Works*, 1:222–24.
49. *Morning Chronicle, and London Advertiser*, 31 December 1787.
50. Mrs. Elizabeth Montagu, *Mrs. Montagu, "Queen of the Blues". Her Letters and Friendships from 1762 to 1800*, ed. Reginald Blunt (London: Constable, 1923), 2:219.
51. Roberts, *Memoirs*, 2:94, 83–84.

Chapter Four

1. James Sutherland, *A Preface to Eighteenth Century Poetry* (Oxford: Clarendon Press, 1948), p. 50.
2. Soame Jenyns, "Poems on Several Occasions," Portland Collection, B.L. Loan MS. 29/326, p. 49.
3. Ibid., p. 13.
4. [Soame Jenyns], *The Art of Dancing. A Poem, In Three Canto's* (London, 1729), p. 7.
5. Ibid., p. 11.
6. Ibid.
7. Ibid., pp. 42–43.
8. Cf. Alexander Pope, *Epistles to Several Persons*, Twickenham Edition of the Poems of Alexander Pope, 2d ed., ed. F. W. Bateson (London: Methuen, 1961), vol. 3, pt. 2, pp. 83 ff., esp. ll. 372, 386, 393–94, 401–2.

9. Cf. William Hogarth, "The Rake's Progress" (1735), plate 5.
10. See Cecil A. Moore, "Shaftesbury and the Ethical Poets of England," in *Backgrounds of English Literature, 1700–1760* (Minneapolis: University of Minnesota Press, 1953), pp. 3–52.
11. John Dryden, *Essays*, ed. W. P. Ker (New York: Russell & Russell, 1961), 1:237.
12. *The Spectator*, ed. Donald F. Bond (Oxford: Clarendon Press, 1965), 5:113.
13. Cumberland, *Memoirs*, p. 247.
14. Cf. Soame Jenyns, *Works* (London, 1790), 1:83 f., esp. ll. 1–6, 45–48, 53–54, 139–43, 233–36.
15. Pope, *Imitations of Horace*, Twickenham Edition, ed. John Butt, 4:229.

Chapter Five

1. B.L. Add. MS. 5832, f. 128.
2. Barclay's Bank Archives, London. Martin's Bank Christmas balance books, 1742–60. Jenyns's pass book is preserved at Bottisham Hall.
3. See, for example, B.L. Add. MSS. 32699, ff. 467–68; 33002, ff. 440–46; 32995, ff. 158–69; 33034, ff. 169–71, 173–81, 183–88, 327–30, 342–50, 351–54, 355–63, 365–72; 51430, ff. 38–43; 32997, ff. 66–67, 101–11.
4. Northamptonshire Record Office, Fitzwilliam MS. 1076/1/9.
5. See J. P. Kenyon, *Revolutionary Principles: The Politics of Party, 1689–1720* (Cambridge, 1977), chap. 1.
6. John Locke, *Two Treatises of Government*, ed. Peter Laslett, 2d ed. (Cambridge: Cambridge University Press, 1967), p. 376.
7. See Willmoore Kendall, *John Locke and the Doctrine of Majority Rule* (Urbana: University of Illinois Press, 1941).
8. *Literary Magazine* 2 (1757):306.
9. Richard Watson, *The Principles of the Revolution vindicated in a Sermon Preached Before the University of Cambridge, on Wednesday, May 29, 1776* (Cambridge, 1776), pp. 7, 11. See also Watson, *Anecdotes*, 1:143.
10. Locke, *Two Treatises*, p. 287.
11. Ibid.
12. Ibid., pp. 350–51.
13. Ibid., p. 385.
14. *The Statutes at Large* (London, 1769–1800), 8:246–54.
15. See J. R. Western, *The English Militia in the Eighteenth*

Notes and References

Century (London, 1965), pp. 131 ff.

16. See especially P. D. G. Thomas, *British Politics and the Stamp Act Crisis* (Oxford, 1975).

17. B.L. Add. MS. 32974, f. 167.

18. For an introduction to the civil conflicts of the 1760s, see Walter J. Shelton's *English Hunger and Industrial Disorders* (London, 1973), especially pt. 1, chap. 2.

19. Ibid., p. 53.

20. "It ought not to be called a Pamphlet," wrote C. N. Cole, "nor to be sold for a shilling. He is angry with Dodsley about the Price he hath fixd it at" (B.L. Add. MS. 35622, f. 213: Cole to Hardwicke, 10 May 1784).

21. Cole in preface to Jenyns, *Works*, 1:x.

Chapter Six

1. For a thorough discussion of the conflict between religion and science, see J. M. Creed and J. S. Boys Smith, *Religious Thought in the Eighteenth Century* (Cambridge: Cambridge University Press, 1934); J. S. Lawton, *Miracles and Revelation* (London: Lutterworth Press, 1959); Robert H. Hurlbutt, *Hume, Newton, and the Design Argument* (Lincoln, 1965); and D. L. LeMahieu, *The Mind of William Paley* (Lincoln, 1976).

2. Joseph Addison, *Works*, ed. George Washington Greene (New York: Putnam, 1856), 1:203.

3. Roberts, *Memoirs*, 1:309–10.

4. William Paley, *Works* (London: Rivington et al., 1819), 3:256.

5. See Andrew Crichton, *Converts from Infidelity* (Edinburgh: Constable and Co., 1827); A. Lamson, "*A View of the Internal Evidence of the Christian Religion*. By Soame Jenyns, Esq. Princeton, N.J.," *Christian Examiner and Theological Review* 3(1826):136–57; "Remarks on the Genius and Writings of Soame Jenyns, Esq. and on the Internal Evidences of Christianity," *Christian Examiner* 3 (1826); and Ritchie J. Ewing, "Soame Jenyns," *Christian World Magazine* 14 (1878):948–56.

6. Cole, "Sketches," p. xxvii.

7. Alexander Pope, *An Essay on Man*, Twickenham Edition, ed. Maynard Mack, vol. 3, pt. 1, p. xxiv.

8. For a full discussion of this philosophical question, see Arthur O. Lovejoy, *The Great Chain of Being* (Cambridge, Mass., 1936) and John Hick, *Evil and the God of Love*, 2d ed. (London, 1977).

9. See Lovejoy, *Great Chain*, pp. 52–61.

10. Pope, *An Essay on Man*, pp. 50–51.
11. *Literary Magazine* 2 (1757):301.
12. Johnson's attitudes to evil are explored by Richard B. Schwartz in *Samuel Johnson and the Problem of Evil* (Madison, 1975), which includes a facsimile of the review. His reviewing technique receives attention in Donald D. Eddy, *Samuel Johnson, Book Reviewer in the Literary Magazine: or, Universal Review* (New York, 1979).
13. *Literary Magazine*, 2 (1757):174, 252, 253.
14. Ibid., 171.
15. See Donald J. Greene, "'Pictures to the Mind': Johnson and Imagery," in *Johnson, Boswell and Their Circle: Essays presented to Lawrence Fitzroy Powell in honour of his eighty-fourth birthday* (Oxford: Clarendon Press, 1965), p. 141.
16. *Literary Magazine* 2 (1757):252.
17. Ibid., 301.
18. For an historical discussion of external evidences in English theology, see Lawton, *Miracles and Revelation*, chap. 4.
19. Paley, *Works*, 3:256.
20. Cf. *Literary Magazine* 2 (1757):302–4, and Jenyns, *Works*, 3:82–92.
21. Boswell, *Boswell's Life of Johnson*, 3:48.
22. The last paragraph of Disquisition II appears almost verbatim in "Reflections on Several Subjects" and Disquisition IV in *Miscellaneous Pieces in Verse and Prose*, pp. 371 ff., as "Philosophical Considerations on the Nature of Time."
23. "Simplex," *Letters Addressed to Soame Jenyns, Esq.* (London, 1791), p. 3.
24. See J. H. Harder, *Observations on Some Tendencies of Sentiment and Ethics Chiefly in Minor Poetry and Essay in the Eighteenth Century Until the Execution of Dr. W. Dodd in 1777* (Amsterdam: Drukkerij M.J. Portielje, 1933), pp. 231 ff.

Selected Bibliography

PRIMARY SOURCES

1. Poetry
The Art of Dancing. A Poem, in Three Canto's. London, 1729.
The Modern Fine Gentleman. London, 1746.
The Modern Fine Lady. London, 1751.
An Ode. London, 1780.
An Ode to the Hon. Philip Y--ke, Esq; Imitated from Horace, Lib. II. Ode XVI. To which is added the same Ode imitated and inscribed to the Earl of B--- on his Creation. London, 1747.
A Simile. London, 1759.
The 'Squire and the Parson: an Eclogue. London, [1749].

2. Essays and Pamphlets
The Objections to the Taxation of Our American Colonies, by the Legislature of Great Britain, Briefly Consider'd. London, 1765.
A Scheme for the Coalition of Parties, Humbly Submitted to the Publick. London, 1772.
Short But Serious Reasons for a National Militia. London, 1757.
Thoughts on a Parliamentary Reform. London, 1784.
Thoughts on the Causes and Consequences of the Present High Price of Provisions. London, 1767.
World. Nos. 125, 153, 157, 163, 178. London, 1753–56.

3. Philosophical Prose
Disquisitions on Several Subjects. London, 1782.
A Free Inquiry into the Nature and Origin of Evil. In Six Letters to -----. London, 1757.
A View of the Internal Evidence of the Christian Religion. London, 1776.

4. Collected Works
Miscellaneous Pieces, in Two Volumes. London, 1761.
Miscellaneous Pieces in Verse and Prose. London, 1770.
Poems. By*****. London, 1752.
The Works of Soame Jenyns, Esq. in Four Volumes. Including Several Pieces Never Before Published. To Which are Prefixed, Short Sketches of the History of the Author's Family, and also of his Life; by Charles Nalson Cole, Esq. London, 1790.

5. Selected Works
[Aikin, John.] *Essays on Song-writing: With a Collection of Such English Songs As Are Most Eminent for Poetical Merit. To Which Are Added, Some Original Pieces.* London, [1772].
The British Poets. Including Translations. Vol. 71. [Edited by R. A. Davenport.] Chiswick: Printed by C. Whittingham for J. Carpenter et al., 1822.
The Cabinet of Poetry, Containing the Best Entire Pieces to be Found in the Works of The British Poets. Edited by Samuel Jackson Pratt. 6 vols. London: Richard Phillips, 1808.
A Collection of Original Scotch Songs, with a Thorough Bass to each Song, for the Harpsichord. London, [1726?].
A Collection of Poems. By Several Hands. [Edited by Robert Dodsley.] 6 vols. London, 1748, 1755, 1758.
A Collection of Poems in Four Volumes. Edited by George Pearch. London, 1770.
A Collection of Scarce, Curious and Valuable Pieces, Both in Verse and Prose; Chiefly Selected from the Fugitive Productions of the Most Eminent Wits of the Present Age. Edinburgh, 1773.
A Companion for a Leisure Hour: being a Collection of Fugitive Pieces, in Prose and Verse. London, 1769.
The Foundling Hospital for Wit. Edited by "Timothy Silence" et al. [Sir Charles Hanbury Williams]. Nos. 1-6. London, 1743, 1744, 1746-49, 1763.
A Collection of Poems. Edited by Sir Charles Hanbury Williams et al. London, 1763.
The Lady's Poetical Magazine, or Beauties of British Poetry. 3 vols. London, 1781, 1782.
The Monitor; a Select Collection of Poems on the Most Important Subjects. London: S. Rousseau, 1808.
The Muse's Mirror. 2 vols. London, 1778.
The Museum: or, the Literary and Historical Register. Edited by Mark Akenside. 3 vols. London, 1746-47.
The New Foundling Hospital for Wit. 6 vols. London, 1784.

Selected Bibliography

Poems by Soame Jenyns, containing "Art of Dancing," "To Lord Lovelace," "Essay on Virtue," "Written in Locke," "Epitaph on Doctor Johnson"; to which is Prefixed a Sketch of the Author's Life. Manchester, 1797.
Poems by Soame Jenyns, Esq. Containing The Art of Dancing and Other Pieces, with the Author's Life. Poughmill near Ludlow: George Nicholson; London: T. Conder et al., 1801.
The Poets of Great Britain. Bell's Edition. Vol. 58. London, 1777–87.
The Poets of Great Britain. Vol. 120. London: Cadell and Davies et al., 1807.
Porson, Richard. *Eloisa in Deshabille: a Satirical Poem.* By the late Professor Porson. To which are added *The Modern Fine Gentleman, Modern Fine Lady, Curtain Lectures,* and *The Squire and the Parson.* 6th ed. London: J. J. Stockdale, 1819.
A Select Collection of Poems, From the most approved Authors. 2 vols. Edinburgh, 1768.
Select Collections of Poems, from Admired Authors, and Scarce Miscellanies. North-Shields, 1790.
The Works of the British Poets. With Prefaces, Biographical and Critical, by Robert Anderson, M.D. Vol. 11. Edinburgh, 1792–95.
The Works of the British Poets, Collated with the Best Editions, by Thomas Park, F.S.A. Vol. 32. London: J. Sharpe, 1808–09.
The Works of the British Poets, with Lives of the Authors. Vol. 32. Edited by Ezekiel Sanford and Robert Walsh, Jr. Philadelphia: Mitchell, Ames, & White, 1819–23.
The Works of the English Poets. With Prefaces, Biographical and Critical. By Samuel Johnson. 2d ed. Vol. 73. London, 1790.
The Works of the English Poets, from Chaucer to Cowper; Including the Series Edited, with Prefaces, Biographical and Critical, by Dr. Samuel Johnson: and the Most Approved Translations. The Additional Lives by Alexander Chalmers, F.S.A. Vol. 17. London: J. Johnson et al., 1810.

6. Contemporary Criticism and Pamphlet Literature

A., F. [James Otis]. *Considerations on Behalf of the Colonists. In a Letter to a Noble Lord.* London, 1765.
An Answer to Thoughts on a Parliamentary Reform. London, 1784.
[Belsham, William.] *Essays, Philosophical, Historical and Literary.* London, 1789.
[Bollan, William.] *The Mutual Interest of Great Britain and the American Colonies Considered, With respect to An Act passed*

last sessions of Parliament for laying a Duty on Merchandise &c. With Some Remarks on a Pamphlet, intitled, "Objections to the Taxation of the American Colonies, &c. considered." In a Letter to a Member of Parliament. London, 1765.

Cartwright, John. *Internal Evidence; Or An Inquiry How Far Truth and the Christian Religion Have Been Consulted by the Author of Thoughts on a Parliamentary Reform.* London, 1784.

———. *The Postscript to Major Cartwright's Reply to Soame Jenyns, Esq; Humbly Recommended to the Perusal of Lord North's Admirers, Previous to His Lordship's Next Speech Against a Parliamentary Reform.* London, 1785.

[Dulany, Daniel.] *Considerations on the Propriety of Imposing Taxes in the British Colonies, For the Purpose of raising a REVENUE, by ACT of PARLIAMENT.* 2d ed. Annapolis, 1765.

An Essay on Valour: Occasioned By the perusal of some Reflections on Valour, in an excellent Performance lately published under the Title of "A View of the internal Evidence of the Christian Religion, by Soame Jenyns, Esq." London, 1776.

Fleet, Edward. *An Address and Reply to the London and Monthly Reviewers.* Oxford, 1777.

———. *An Examination of the Arguments Contained in Dr. Maclaine's Answer to Soame Jenyns, Esq. on his View of the Internal Evidence of the Christian Religion. With General Thoughts and Reflections thereon.* London, 1777.

[Fothergill, John?] *Reflexions on Representation in Parliament: Being An Attempt to shew the Equity and Practicability, not only of establishing a more equal Representation throughout Great Britain, but also of admitting the Americans to a Share in the Legislature: with An Enumeration of the principal Benefits which would result from these Measures, both to the Colonies and the Mother-Country. The Whole submitted to the Consideration of the Public in general, and Members of Parliament in particular; before the Final Determination of the present Disputes. With some Strictures on a Pamphlet, intitled, "Objections to the Taxation of the Colonies by the Legislature of Great Britain briefly considered."* London, 1766.

Gentle Reflections upon the Short but Serious Reasons for a National Militia. London, 1757.

Kenrick, William. *Observations on Soame Jenyns's View of the Internal Evidence of the Christian Religion; Addressed to its*

Almost-Christian Author. London, 1776.

Latuit [William Jesse]. *Lectures Supposed to have been Delivered by the Author of a View of the Internal Evidence of the Christian Religion, to a Select Company of Friends.* Dedicated to Edward Gibbon, Esq. London, 1787.

A letter to Soame Jenyns, Esq. wherein the Futility and Absurdity of Some Part of his Reasoning in his View of the Internal Evidence of the Christian Religion, is Set Forth and Exposed. By a Clergyman of the Church of England. London, 1776.

A Letter to the Author of a Free Enquiry into the Nature and Origin of Evil; Containing Remarks on the four first Letters of that Enquiry. London, [1759].

Literary Magazine: or, Universal Review. 3 vols. London, 1756–58. Johnson's review of the *Free Inquiry* appears in 2 (1757):171–75, 251–53, and 301–6.

London Review of English and Foreign Literature. 11 vols. London, 1775–80. Reviews of *A View of the Internal Evidence* by William Kenrick and reviews of other publications replying to Jenyns appear as follows: 3:508–28; 4:131–39, 150–57, 160–69, 225–29, 240, 308–14, 317, 479–80, 488, 534–39; 5:340–47, 443–47, 457–62; 6:197–200, 455–56.

[Lowe, George.] *Considerations on the Effects which the Bounties Granted on Exported Corn, Malt, and Flour, have on the Manufactures of the Kingdom, and the True Interests of the State.* With a postscript containing remarks on a pamphlet lately published, intituled *Thoughts on the Causes and Consequences of the Present High Price of Provisions.* London, 1768.

MacGreggor, Malcolm [William Mason]. *The Dean and the 'Squire: a Political Eclogue.* Humbly dedicated to Soame Jenyns, Esq. By the Author of the Heroic Epistle to Sir William Chambers, &c. London, 1782.

Maclaine, Archibald. *A Series of Letters, Addressed to Soame Jenyns, Esq; on Occasion of his View of the Internal Evidence of Christianity.* London, 1777.

[Morgan, Caesar.] *Thoughts on a Pre-existent State, in Answer to a Late Disquisition on That Subject.* Cambridge, 1782.

[Peck, Samuel?] *An Answer to a Pamphlet Intitled, "Thoughts on the Causes and Consequences of the present high Price of Provisions:" in a Letter, Addressed To the supposed Author of that Pamphlet.* By A Gentleman of Cambridge. London, 1768.

Philagathos [Caleb Fleming]. *Necessity, not the origin of evil, religious or moral. A Letter to the Ingenious Author of a Free*

Inquiry into the Nature and Origin of Evil. London, 1757.
Philosophical Disquisitions on the Christian Religion Addressed to Soame Jenyns, Esq. and W. Kenrick, L.L.D. London, 1777.
[Shepherd, Richard.] *Letters to Soame Jenyns, Esq; Occasioned by his Free Enquiry into the Nature and Origin of Evil. To Which are Added, Three Discourses. I. On Conscience. II. On Inspiration. III. On a Paradisiacal State.* Oxford, 1768.
———. *The Review of a Free Enquiry into the Nature and Origin of Evil.* London, 1759.
Short Strictures on Certain Passages in A View of the Internal Evidence of the Christian Religion, By Soame Jenyns, Esq. Written by a Layman. London, 1776.
Simplex [John Young]. *Letters Addressed to Soame Jenyns, Esq. Containing Strictures on the Writings of Edward Gibbon, Esq; Dr. Priestley, Mr. Theophilus Lindsay, &c. &c. and an Abstract of Dr. Priestley's Account Current with Revelation. With a Preface, or, what may be called the Reviewers Reviewed.* London, 1791.
Some Other Thoughts on a Parliamentary Reform; in Reply to a Late Publication, Entitled, "Thoughts on a Parliamentary Reform." London, 1784.
Stockdale, Percival. *Six Discourses; to which is Prefixed an Introduction; Containing A View of the Genuine Ancient Philosophy; of the natural, and effectual Tendency of that Philosophy, and of Christian Morality, to all True Prosperity in this World; and some Observations on a Book Lately Published, Entitled, a View of the Internal Evidence of the Christian Religion.* London, 1777.
[Taylor, Henry.] *A Full Answer to a Late View of the Internal Evidence of the Christian Religion. In a Dialogue between a Rational Christian and his Friend.* By the Editor of Ben Mordecai's Letters to Elisha Levi. London, 1777.
Turner, Baptist Noel. *Candid Suggestions; in Eight Letters to Soame Jenyns, Esq; on the Respective Subjects of his Disquisitions, Lately Published: with some Remarks on the Answerer of his Seventh Disquisition, Respecting the Principles of Mr. Locke.* London, 1782.
U., G. *A Letter to Soame Jenyns, Esq; Occasioned by an Assertion Contained in his View of the Internal Evidence of the Christian Religion.* London, 1776.
[Watson, Richard.] *An Answer to the Disquisition on Government and Civil Liberty; in a Letter to the Author of Disquisitions on Several Subjects.* London, 1782.

Selected Bibliography

SECONDARY SOURCES

Basye, Arthur Herbert. *The Lords Commissioners of Trade and Plantations, Commonly Known as the Board of Trade, 1748-1782.* New Haven: Yale University Press, 1925. A study of the board's activities, beginning with the presidency of Lord Halifax, including a record of attendance.
Brewer, John. *Party Ideology and Popular Politics at the Accession of George III.* Cambridge: Cambridge University Press, 1976. Raises questions about the political society of the eighteenth century and the role of ideology in politics.
Brown, Stuart Gerry. "Dr. Johnson and the Old Order." *Marxist Quarterly* 1 (1937):418-30. Argues that in his review of the *Free Inquiry*, Johnson contradicts himself and is not always sure which position to take in criticizing Jenyns's defense of the status quo at a time when the proletarian struggle against the landed and merchant classes had begun to accelerate.
Cam, Helen. "*Quo Warranto* Proceedings at Cambridge 1780-1790." *Cambridge Historical Journal* 8 (1946):145-65. Traces, in part, the pattern of political influence in Cambridge during the eighteenth century.
Cannon, John. *Parliamentary Reform, 1640-1832.* Cambridge: Cambridge University Press, 1973. An examination of reform movements from the parliament of 1640 to the Great Reform Bill, with special reference to reform activities in Parliament itself.
Christie, Ian R. *Wilkes, Wyvill and Reform.* London: Macmillan, 1962. Analyzes the agitation for parliamentary reform in the early years of George III's reign by considering the scale of the movement, the types of personalities, the kinds of ideas generated, and the impact made on the population.
Clarke, Mary P. "The Board of Trade at Work." *American Historical Review* 17 (1911):17-42. Examines the organization of the Board of Trade offices and the nature of the business transacted there.
Cook, Daniel. "The Representative History of the County, Town and University of Cambridge, 1689-1832." Ph.D. dissertation, London University, 1935. Traces the nature of representation and the power structure in the county from the beginning of the reign of William and Mary to the Great Reform Bill and includes biographical notes on the representatives.
Dickinson, H. T. *Liberty and Property: Political Ideology in*

Eighteenth-Century Britain. London: Weidenfield and Nicolson, 1977. A study of the relationship between political ideas and political action from the 1680s to the 1790s, emphasizing the structure of political ideas and arguments, especially the distinction between Whig and Tory.

Eddy, Donald D. *Samuel Johnson, Book Reviewer in the Literary Magazine: or, Universal Review 1756–1758.* New York: Garland Publishing, 1979. Largely bibliographical treatment of Johnson as a reviewer, with some analysis of his reviewing techniques.

Hailstone, Edward. *The History and Antiquities of the Parish of Bottisham and the Priory of Anglesey in Cambridgeshire.* Cambridge Antiquarian Society, Octavo Publications, no. 14. Cambridge: Deighton, Bell & Co., 1873. Supplement, 1878. Sometimes untrustworthy, but the only attempt to account for the activities of the Jenyns family in Cambridgeshire.

Hick, John. *Evil and the God of Love.* 2d ed. London: Macmillan, 1977. Within the context of Christian faith, a thorough critical study of responses to the problem of evil that have developed within Christian thought, with a view to constructing a theodicy for contemporary life. Includes a chapter on eighteenth-century optimism.

Hurlbutt, Robert H. *Hume, Newton, and the Design Argument.* Lincoln: University of Nebraska Press, 1965. While discussing Newton's theism and laying out the progress of the design argument from classical thought, this book deals with the interrelationship between science and theology at a time of great intellectual ferment and the subsequent impact of natural theology.

Kenyon, J. P. *Revolution Principles: The Politics of Party, 1689–1720.* Cambridge: Cambridge University Press, 1977. Discusses the evolution of Whig and Tory political ideas under William III and Queen Anne and demonstrates that constitutional theories advanced by defenders of the Revolution did not at this time follow closely those of Locke.

LeMahieu, D. L. *The Mind of William Paley.* Lincoln: University of Nebraska Press, 1976. While analyzing the thought of William Paley, a clear account of the intellectual tradition in which he wrote.

Lovejoy, Arthur O. *The Great Chain of Being.* Cambridge, Mass.: Harvard University Press, 1936. An attempt at a definitive history of this idea from its beginnings in classical thought.

Pearson, Norman. "A Male Blue-stocking: Soame Jenyns." *Nineteenth Century* 62 (1907):126–41. The best short article available on Jenyns, viewing him as an eccentric both in his personal habits and in his thought.

Rompkey, Ronald. "Soame Jenyns, M.P.: A Curious Case of Membership." *Journal of the Royal Society of Arts* 120 (1972):536–42. Documents Jenyns's membership in the Society of Arts and attempts to identify his likeness in the mural "Human Culture," by James Barry, which adorns the Society's hall.

―――. "Some Uncollected Authors XLIX: Soame Jenyns." *Book Collector* 25 (1976):210–24. Descriptive bibliography of Jenyns's first editions.

Schwartz, Richard B. *Samuel Johnson and the Problem of Evil.* Madison: University of Wisconsin Press, 1975. An examination of Johnson's writings on the problem of evil, with particular reference to his review of Jenyns's *Free Inquiry*, which is printed in facsimile.

Shelton, Walter J. *English Hunger and Industrial Disorders.* London: Macmillan, 1973. A study of the economic context and underlying social causes that produced the riots taking place in the first decade of George III's reign.

Thomas, P. D. G. *British Politics and the Stamp Act Crisis.* Oxford: Clarendon Press, 1975. Focuses on the political context of the Stamp Act and the step-by-step process of its enactment and repeal.

Western, J. R. *The English Militia in the Eighteenth Century.* London: Routledge & Kegan Paul, 1965. A study of the formation of public opinion in the eighteenth century as it was related to the role of the militia, a constant source of debate in national politics and local government.

Williams, Basil. "The Eclipse of the Yorkes." *Transactions of the Royal Historical Society*, 3d ser. 2 (1908):129–51. Conveys the sense of tragedy arising out of a great political family's failure and loss of honor, 1760–70.

Index

Addison, Joseph, 131

Bacon, John, R.A., 70
Badcock, Rev. Samuel, 59
Banks, Sir Joseph, 49
Barbauld, Mrs. Anna Letitia, 62
Barry, James, 66
Beattie, James, 56
Bedford Level Corporation, 1–2
Birch, Thomas, 24
Bluestockings, 46, 49, 66–70
Board of Trade, 27–30
Boscawen, Mrs., 46, 68
Boswell, James, 22, 26, 33, 35, 53, 56, 57
Bottisham, Cambridgeshire, 3, 110
Bottisham Hall (Jenyns estate), 3
Bowles, William, 25
Bromley, Henry, 10–11
Brown, Rev. John, 23–24
Browne, Isaac Hawkins, 90–91
Brydges, Sir Egerton, 16
Burke, Edmund, 30, 43, 47
Burney, Dr. Charles, 22, 69
Burney, Fanny, 68–69
Burgh, William, 64, 65
Butler, Bishop Joseph, 53, 145
Byde, Thomas Plumer, 50–52

Cadogan, Charles Sloane, 37, 42, 43, 50–52
Cambridge, Richard Owen, 21, 68
Cambridge, George, 69
Cambridge, town of, 49–52

Cambridge University, 4–5
Carter, Mrs. Elizabeth, 56
Cartwright, Major John, 48
Chesterfield, fourth earl of, 49
Cheveley, 16
Cole, Charles Nalson, 3, 4, 55, 134, 169n20
Cole, Rev. William (of Milton), 3, 6, 7, 8, 11, 18, 19, 50, 51, 100, 159
Courtney, John, 26
Cumberland, Richard, 18–19, 19–20, 30, 68, 92

Deists, 131–32, 134
Denham, Sir John, 87
Dobson, Susanna, 68
Dodsley, Robert, 12, 13–14, 15–16, 34, 55, 169; his *Collection*, 14, 72–73, 74, 80, 86, 89, 90
Downing, Sir Jacob, 18, 36–37
Dryden, John, 86, 92
Dulany, Daniel, 39

Edmundson, Dr. William, 4
Enfield, William, 61

Fleet, Rev. Edward, 60
Fleming, Caleb, 33, 140
Forbes, Sir William, 56
Fothergill, John, 40
Fox, Charles James, 164n30
Franklin, Benjamin, 21

Gay, John, 81, 86
Gibbon, Edward, 30

Index

Granby, marquis of, 16, 17, 18
Gray, Thomas, 14, 15, 25, 33, 64, 65
Grenville, George, 38, 40
Griffiths, Ralph, 15, 16, 60

Halifax, second earl of, 28, 29
Hamilton, Gerard, 32
Hardwicke, first earl of, 10, 17, 24, 36, 37, 38, 40, 96, 97, 99, 101, 116
Hardwicke, second earl of (Philip Yorke), 10, 12, 45, 70, 93
Henry, Patrick, 55
Hill, Rev. W., 4
Hobbes, Thomas, 115
Holland, third baron, 67
Horace, 92, 93, 94, 95, 96, 97
Hume, David, 33, 35, 53
Hutchinson, Thomas, 55

Jenyns, Lady Elizabeth (mother), 3-4, 7
Jenyns, Elizabeth (second wife), 7-8
Jenyns, John (uncle), 2
Jenyns, Martha (Sir Roger's first wife), 3
Jenyns, Mary (first wife), 7
Jenyns, Roger (grandfather), 2
Jenyns, Sir Roger (father), 2-3, 7, 9
Jenyns, Soame: birth, 4; youth, 4; education, 4-5; first marriage, 7; second marriage, 7; enters politics, 11; political career, 100-101; portrait, 18-26; as pamphleteer, 35-49; his Christianity, 53, 133-34; his even temper, 67-68; his death, 70

WORKS—POETRY:
"American Coachman, The," 46, 109
"Anacreon, Ode 20, a free Translation," 79
"Art of Dancing, The," 6, 81-84
"Choice, The," 79
"De Animi Immortalitate," 90-91
"Dialogue Between the Right Hon. Henry Pelham and Madam Popularity, A," 94-95
"Epistle, Written in the Country, to the Right Hon. the Lord Lovelace then in Town, An," 8, 12, 84-86, 150
"Epitaph on Dr. Samuel Johnson," 25, 26, 162
"Essay on Virtue, An," 14, 89-90, 133, 138, 139, 157
"First Epistle of the Second Book of Horace, Imitated, The," 14, 95-99, 132
"Horace, Book IV. Ode VIII. Imitated," 94
"Modern Fine Gentleman, The," 11-12, 74, 86-87, 158
"Modern Fine Lady, The," 15, 74, 86, 88
"Ode, An," 24-25, 64
"Ode to the Hon. Philip Yorke, An," 13, 93-94
"On the Marchioness of Carmarthen's Recovery from the Small Pox," 77
"Picture, The," 6
Poems. By *****, 15-16
"Poems on Several Occasions. Dedicated to the Rt. Hon. the Lady Margaret

Cavendish Harley," 6, 12, 72–73, 75
"Simile, A," 23–24
"Song, A," 79–80
"'Squire and the Parson, The," 14–15
"Temple of Venus, The," 80
"To a Lady, in Answer to a Letter Wrote in a Very Fine Hand," 78
"To a Lady in Town, Soon After Her Leaving the Country," 5–6, 77–78
"To a Lady, Sent with a Present of Shells and Stones Designed for a Grotto," 78
"To a Nosegay in Pancharilla's Breast," 79
"To a Young Lady, Going to the West Indies," 78
"Way to be Wise, The," 78–79
"Written in a Lady's Volume of Tragedies," 78
"Written in His Grace the Duke of Buckingham's Works," 76–77
"Written in Mr. Locke's Essay on Human Understanding," 78
"Written in the Right Honourable the Earl of Oxford's Library at Wimple," 75–76

WORKS—PROSE:
Disquisitions on Several Subjects, 61–66, 110–15, 138, 139, 148–53, 157–58
Free Inquiry into the Nature and Origin of Evil, A, 31–35, 56, 104–107, 133, 134–43, 149, 157

Objections to the Taxation of Our American Colonies, by the Legislature of Great Britain, Briefly Considered, The, 38–40, 118–21
"Reflections on Several Subjects," 107–10
Scheme for the Coalition of Parties, A, 44, 123–25
Short But Serious Reasons for a National Militia, 36, 116–18
Thoughts on a Parliamentary Reform, 47–48, 125–27
Thoughts on the Causes and Consequences of the Present High Price of Provisions, 41–42, 121–23
"*Thoughts on the National Debt*," 49, 127–28
View of the Internal Evidence of the Christian Religion, A, 53–61, 48, 133, 139, 143–48, 157, 158
World no. 125, 109, 122
World no. 163, 31, 138, 150, 151
World no. 177, 5
World no. 178, 31

Johnson, Samuel, 18, 22–23, 25–26, 57, 67, 105, 146; review of the *Free Inquiry*, 34–35, 140–43
Jones, Rev. William (of Nayland), 56
"Junius," 124

Kenrick, William, 58–59, 60
King, Archbishop William, 135

Index

Leibniz, Gottfried Wilhelm von, 135
Levinz, William, 7
Locke, John: *Two Treatises of Government*, 62–63, 65, 102–103, 109, 110–15
Lords Commissioners of Trade and Plantations, The. *See* Board of Trade
Lowe, George, 42

Maclaine, Rev. Archibald, 59, 60
Mainwaring, Rev. John, 59
Malone, Edmond, 18, 20, 56
Manners family. *See* Granby
Mason, William, 22, 25, 64–66, 68
Meeke, Samuel, 50–52
Militia Bill, 35–36, 115–16
Montagu, Mrs. Elizabeth, 66, 67, 68, 70
Montague, Edward Wortley, 35
Montfort, first lord, 17, 43
More, Hannah, 20, 67, 68, 70, 133
Morgan, Caesar, 62

Natural religion, 130–32
Newcastle, first duke of, 10, 18, 34, 37, 38, 100
Nichols, John, 55
North, Lord Frederick, second earl of Guilford, 43

Ord, Mrs., 69
Otis, James, 39–40, 120
Oxford, first earl of, 75, 76

Paley, William, 132, 134, 144
Parliamentary reform, 44, 47–48, 49–52, 56–57, 62–63, 65, 103, 108–109, 110–15, 125–27, 152–53

Peck, Rev. Samuel, 41–42
Pelham, Henry, 94–95, 100
Philips, Ambrose, 92
Piozzi, Mrs. Hester. *See* Thrale
Pitt, William (the elder), 23, 24, 27, 34, 36, 41, 116
Pitt, William (the younger), 47, 127
Pomfret, John, 79
Pope, Alexander, 14, 33, 76, 77, 81, 82, 85, 86, 92, 96, 97, 99, 134, 135, 138, 141, 142
Prior, Matthew, 74–75, 76, 79, 85

Rees, Abraham, 57
Reynolds, Joshua, 19
Rockingham, second marquis of, 40–41, 124
Rose, William, 33

St. Augustine, 135
St. John's College, Cambridge, 4–5, 74
Scott, Rev. Thomas, 56
Shaftesbury, third earl of, 89
Shepheard, Samuel, 10–11, 12
Shepherd, Richard, 33, 140
Sheridan, Elizabeth, 19
Sheridan, Thomas, 68
Smith, Adam, 35, 129
Soame, Col. Edmond (father-in-law), 7
Soame, Sir Peter (grandfather), 3, 7
Society for the Encouragement of Arts, Manufacturers and Commerce, The, 49, 66
Stamp Act, 38, 118–19
Stockdale, Percival, 60
Swift, Jonathan, 76

Taylor, Rev. Henry, 60
Thrale, Mrs. Hester (later Piozzi), 15, 22, 26, 55, 69
Trumpington, 50–52
Tucker, Josiah, dean of Gloucester, 45–46, 65
Turner, Rev. Baptist Noel, 63

Vesey, Mrs. Elizabeth, 19, 68

Walpole, Horace, 13, 19, 21, 22, 24, 25, 28–29, 56, 62, 64–66, 67, 68, 99

Watson, Richard, bishop of Llandaff, 63, 110, 114
Weales, William, 43, 50
Wesley, John, 57
Whig party, 100
White, Rev. Stephen, 4
Wilkes, John, 44, 47, 107, 124–25
Wimpole Hall, 10, 75, 76, 99
World, The, 30–31

Yorke family. *See* Hardwicke
Young, John, 149